HOW
TO SELL
YOUR
IDEAS

By the same author

Getting Through to People
Breaking Through to Each Other

HOW TO SELL YOUR IDEAS

Jesse S. Nirenberg, Ph.D.

McGRAW-HILL PUBLISHING COMPANY

NEW YORK   ST. LOUIS   SAN FRANCISCO   AUCKLAND   BOGOTÁ
CARACAS   HAMBURG   LISBON   LONDON   MADRID   MEXICO
MILAN   MONTREAL   NEW DELHI   OKLAHOMA CITY   PARIS
SAN JUAN   SÃO PAULO   SINGAPORE   SYDNEY   TOKYO   TORONTO

To my wife, Edna,
our daughters, Liz, Sheila, and Nina,
our sons-in-law, Tom Brondolo and Steve Youngstrom,
and our granddaughter, Emma.

First paperback edition 1989

1 2 3 4 5 6 7 8 9 FGR FGR 8 9 3 2 1 0 9

ISBN 0-07-046580-0

LIBRARY OF CONGRESS CATALOGING IN PUBLICATION DATA
   Nirenberg, Jesse S.
   How to sell your ideas.
   Includes index.
1. Selling.   2. Interpersonal communication.
I. Title
HF5438.25.N57   1984   650.1'3   83-19556
ISBN 0-07-046580-0

Book design by Virginia M. Soulé

Contents

Introduction

If making sense were all that's needed to sell good ideas, the world would be a much happier, more productive place. Unfortunately, there's too much unreasonable resistance to others' ideas, and too many communication barriers, to be able to persuade with logic alone.

It takes special techniques to shepherd an idea through all the obstacles so that it comes alive in people's minds. It requires patience and sensitivity, as well as close listening, hard thinking, and clear communicating, to coax others to drop their resistance and to enlist their natural drive toward reasonableness. At the same time, you have to watch that you're not unreasonably resisting others' objections. Otherwise, you'll have mutual resistance and an adversary interaction.

It doesn't help much to *resolve* to do all of these things. There are just too many of them to keep in mind simultaneously. And it's too difficult to stay calm and thoughtful when you're frustrated by others' imperviousness to your reasoning.

But suppose by following certain persuasion methods you automatically listened carefully, did the necessary close analysis of objections, set aside your own resistance and lowered others' defensiveness, and got them to grasp your ideas firmly. And while doing so you maintained high credibility and rapport.

What if by following a set of technique models you could get others to want to know more, to think along with you in a reasonable way, and to judge your ideas on their merits? Your discussions would be partnerships in evaluating benefits and in working out solutions to problems.

Compare this with the very common futile exchange of unresponsive arguing that frequently contains faulty reasoning and wishful thinking, where no one listens and each waits impatiently for his turn to talk. Failure in persuading occurs because each thinks that if he can just outlogic others, he will convince them.

This book was written to give both a unified understanding of the various subtle forces that undermine persuading, and a set of practical techniques to be used to accomplish a successful selling of your ideas. These concepts and techniques are based on twenty-five years of developing persuasive communication skills in managers, professionals, technical specialists, and sales representatives, in many leading companies and government agencies.

The readers are invited to embark on a voyage of both discovery and skill attainment. The intention is to sensitize people to see things they've not been aware of, to help them make new connections, to have them appreciate the complexity of getting others to change their thinking, and above all to impart the skills needed to sell good ideas.

In this book, the techniques are progressively integrated to form a cohesive method. Separate chapters show how to apply this method to selling ideas in a one-to-one interaction, in writing, in negotiating, and to groups. Just about every point is illustrated by a case dialogue or an example.

You'll come to see why in selling your ideas you miss critical points in others' thinking so that what you're saying doesn't fit their immediate concerns. You'll learn how to motivate listening, and to use one of the most powerful tools in persuading—the question—to gain and give insight, to guide others' thinking, and to get them to face facts.

You'll find out how to identify and bring out reasoning

errors in objections, in a supportive way so that others drop their objections and move on without becoming defensive. You'll gain techniques for getting others to absorb and think about the case you're making so that they reason along with you to your conclusion. And you'll combine all of these and other techniques to achieve a smooth-flowing, conflict-resolving interaction.

If you practice this method, you'll draw more fully on your capabilities of analyzing, creating, and listening actively. You'll respond productively to others' feelings while tuning in on your own. And you'll inquire gently and reasonably into others' thinking and get them to absorb yours, and to buy your ideas.

Here's wishing you great success in selling your good ideas. The more you sell, the more we all gain.

‖ 1 ‖ Planning for Persuasion

Expect Resistance

People resist even the best of ideas. The great ideas now prevailing in our culture were bitterly fought for against violent opposition. For many of them blood was spilled. You have to sell your ideas no matter how good they are.

A person resists an idea for a number of reasons. His resistance starts with a negative feeling about the idea. He hasn't looked into it yet. His immediate resistance is general. First of all, there's the risk. What if the idea doesn't pay off? Then, he loses the cost and looks foolish.

Also, an idea means some change. And maybe the change will be uncomfortable. It'll cause trouble, and who needs trouble?

Then there's something about your idea that bothers him but he can't put his finger on it. It just feels wrong. Somehow it seems as though he tried something like it before and it didn't work out well.

Besides, he feels that he could think of a better idea than

yours to serve the same purpose, and whatever your idea is, it would need his improvements, and he's busy with other things.

All this makes him feel that he doesn't want to hear about your idea. But even if you get him to listen, his generalized resistance adds strength to his specific objections. And these take careful handling.

So you're going to have to plan thoroughly, present clearly, listen closely, motivate sensitively, reason soundly, be pleasantly assertive, and deal patiently if you want to do a top job of selling your ideas.

Now, you're probably thinking, if I could do all that, I'd be President. Well, maybe you will be. At least you'll get a lot further in whatever you do if you follow the system in this book. And you'll be doing all these things automatically that seem so impossible at first.

You need to sell your ideas to get ahead. Your talent can't be known unless your good ideas are tried. Their success means your success.

The High Cost of Unsupported Enthusiasm

A lot of people ruin their credibility because they start to sell an idea when it's only half-formed. The germ of the idea is there, and it generates enough enthusiasm in its creator to propel him prematurely into the boss's office.

The boss, motivated by his generalized resistance to any idea, looks for what's wrong with the idea. At this point, he isn't focusing on what's right or on how to make it work. So he raises some tough questions that our hero can't answer. He isn't prepared. His idea dies. He doesn't realize that enthusiasm isn't contagious unless you've got the answers.

But he's lost more than a good idea. He's lost some credibility. He's hurt his image. From then on the boss expects this person to be unprepared. What he says is suspect. The boss looks hard for holes. And he's a little impatient because he figures that maybe he's wasting time. If he hears unsupported ideas, the boss won't listen anymore, especially when this person is enthusiastic.

Keep in mind that everything you say and do affects your image. And each person reacts to you not according to the "real" you, whoever that is, but based on his image of you. And each person has a different image of you, which depends not only on his experience with you, but on what he makes of these experiences. For him to be sold by your ideas, he has to see you as being competent and credible.

Intriguing Concept of Why

The *Why* part of what we know is both fascinating and difficult to find. The Why part of a murder is the motive for it. But the motive is a succession of answers to Why questions. The murderer killed the victim because the victim ran off with the murderer's wife. But why did the murderer not kill his wife since she abandoned him? Because he thought he could get her back. But why did he think that, when in addition to her being willing to leave him, he had become a murderer?

Here we could go on and on because this Why trail leads through the labyrinth of human motivation. All scientific research is a pursuit of answers to Why.

Because Why can call for several layers of answers, and because these questions can be intrusive, people often evade answering them. When reporters asked Willie Sutton, the notorious bank robber, why he robbed banks, he replied, "Because that's where the money is." He didn't answer the question. The reporters were really asking why he was willing to give up a normal life in society, spend so much time in prison if he were captured, and perhaps get killed or hurt badly if he were caught in the act. They were asking about his deeper motivations. Sir

Edmund Hillary, the famous mountain climber, said something similar. When asked why he climbed Mount Everest, he replied, "Because it is there."

The reporters didn't realize that their questions were too difficult to answer. They did know that almost any answer about motivations by someone who takes great risks makes good copy. So readers were amused and relished telling others these non-answers. Possibly, neither Hillary nor Sutton knew the real answers; or if they did, couldn't have told them. How much self-insight can men of action articulate to the world?

Your child asks, "Why do things fall down when there's nothing to hold them up?" You answer, "Because of gravity." You haven't answered the question. You've only said, in effect, because that's what always happens. But he wants to know why it always happens. Scientists are still trying to answer that one.

Not getting anywhere with that question, your child tries another. "Why do some people become engineers, and others, police officers?" You respond, "Because people have different abilities and interests." But he knows that. He wants to know how they got that way. So he gives up and turns to something that offers more satisfaction, like making himself a five-layered sandwich and trying to get all five layers into his mouth in the same bite. But because children want to know why so badly, if you hang around he's likely to ask, "Why can't my mouth open wider?"

Suppose you were asked, "Why do women have babies?" Is the answer, "Because they have sex"; or is it, "Because they want to be mothers"; or is it, "To replenish the population"?

All of these might be true and any one could be the answer wanted, depending on the context of the conversation. If you don't provide the answer that matches the intent of the question, your image is hurt. It sounds as though you're either evading or can't think usefully.

Now, I'm going to give you four Why rules. These are basic and powerful tools for persuading. If you use them, you'll sell a lot more of your ideas.

RULE 1: Never Suggest an Action Without Telling Its End Benefit

We're talking about immediate answers versus end answers to Why. What's this got to do with selling your ideas? A lot. Suppose you say to your spouse, "Let's buy a piano." That's the idea you want to sell. Whenever you want to sell an idea, you've got to answer the question of why you want to do it, before it's even asked. This answer is the benefits. You add, "So the children can learn to play."

That answer is in the same class as Willie Sutton's "Because that's where the money is." Your spouse already knows that having a piano means you can learn to play it. The next Why is, Why do you want them to learn to play the piano? You think a little further and now you say, "So the children can learn to get pleasure from music and can entertain others." But entertaining others raises the further question, Why do you want that? One more step leads you to "So they'll be more popular with others."

The fascinating thing about this is that as you keep moving toward the end Why and its answer, the persuasive impact is higher for each successive answer to Why. "They can learn to play" has a little persuasive impact, "They can entertain others" has still more, and "They'll be more popular with others" has the most. It's on a par with "They can learn to get pleasure from music," which doesn't raise any further Why. You're at the end answer to Why for that result, and you can add it to the other end answer to Why, "So they'll be more popular with others." These are the end benefits.

Before you make any suggestion, think ahead to the end benefits, and always tell them with your suggestion.

*RULE 2: When People Disagree with You, Explore the Reasons
    for Their Objection*

This is the hardest rule to apply, but the one with the biggest
payoff. It's hard because the strong natural impulse is to answer
the objection immediately to get it out of the way. And the better
your argument against the objection is, the greater your temptation to use it to overcome the objection.

The trouble is, the other person isn't listening well. He's
thinking about what he's going to say next to buttress his objection. That often leaves you talking to yourself.

You'd be startled if you knew how often people are really
talking to themselves in conversation. They're polite enough not
to talk at the same time as others do; they take turns in making
remarks to themselves. While each is talking, the other is thinking his own thoughts. Together, they create the illusion of mental interaction by staying on the same general topic.

To link the other person's thinking with yours, you've got
to ask him a question about his objection. You have to inquire
into his reasoning.

Suppose you're trying to get someone to do a job in a different way from the way he'd always been doing it. He'd save
some time if he did.

He replies, "That's too complicated. The way I'm doing it
is easy for me to handle."

How can you answer that objection if you don't know what
the other person means or how he arrived at it? Often, when a
person says his objection, he isn't sure himself what he means.
A word floats by in his mind that seems to express the vague
uneasiness he feels about your idea, so he uses the word.

Or, frequently, he does know what he means, and the words
he uses are accurate, but the reasoning that led him to his words
is wrong.

In this case, does he really mean that the new procedure is
"complicated" in that there are more steps to take, and that

perhaps these steps themselves are more intricate; or is he expressing a feeling that having to learn a new procedure demands concentration and means going through feeling awkward and making more mistakes as he learns the new procedure?

And if he does literally think it is more complicated, why does he think so? Is he misunderstanding it? And if so, what about it is he misunderstanding? Also, is he skeptical about the benefit, or underestimating it, and therefore thinks it's not worth the effort? If you answer his objection without knowing the answers to these questions, aren't you really talking to yourself? You're just answering what you imagine is in his mind.

Another advantage of inquiring into an objection rather than arguing against it is that you're not making the other person your adversary. When you argue with someone, it brings up the feeling of matching wits, of competing. She wants to win, and this might cause her to contrive arguments that don't make sense, or to evade answering to your points. She might even become irritable if your points are stronger than hers. But when you inquire, you suggest that you're trying to solve the problem with her of what to do about your idea. This makes both of you more relaxed.

Questions are powerful, versatile tools. You can do many things with them. You can uncover information, prod the other person to think about something, bring out his feelings, give him new realizations by asking him to reconcile his idea with conflicting facts, check on whether he really means what he says, find out his reactions to your ideas, move him to evaluate, and get commitments. You can shepherd his reasoning, get him to think imaginatively with "what if" questions, and give him insights.

If you develop skill in using questions, you can do great things in both persuading and counseling. For success in both of these depends on getting the other person to see relationships he hadn't seen before.

*RULE 3: Whenever You Ask a Question, Say Why You're
        Asking*

When your question stands alone, it often raises another question in the other person's mind: Why are you asking it? And whenever a person has a question in her mind, she doesn't wait for the answer. Her drive toward closure causes her to think of possible answers, and wonder which it is. She then may assume it's the one that seems most likely to her.

A boss asks an employee, "When will you be finished with the job you're working on?" The employee might wonder: Does he think I'm too slow? or, Does he have something else he wants me to do? or, Is he trying to figure out how long this kind of job takes so he can plan better next time?

In addition to possibly jumping to the wrong conclusion about why the boss is asking, the employee doesn't know how to answer the question. If the employee knew that the boss thinks the employee is working too slowly, he could add that he learned a lot in doing the job and could probably do it faster next time, or that there were unexpected delays. If, on the other hand, the boss had added that he has something in mind for the employee to do after he finishes, and the employee has something else that's urgent to do after this job, he would add that to his answer.

A husband asks his wife, "What time will you be home for dinner?" She wonders: Does he have something else to do before dinner, and he wants to see if he'll have enough time to do it, or does he have something in mind to do after dinner and he wants to see if we'll be able to, or are others coming for dinner, and he wants to know what time to tell them to come. The wife might have changed her time for coming home if she knew why her husband asked.

In addition to causing misunderstandings, your not giving your reason when you ask a question can have two other harmful side effects. First, it can irritate other people if they don't see why you're asking. They might feel cross-examined, especially if there are several such mysterious questions. Second, it can make you feel anxious. Since asking a question is a demand for information, if you feel uncomfortable making demands, you are likely to shy away from asking questions, which will hurt the selling of your idea.

But telling why you're asking, both removes the cross-examination effect and makes you feel more comfortable in making your demand. You are giving something in return in giving your reason for asking. And you are making the other person a partner in your thinking.

When you ask a question, think of it as being incomplete unless you add why you're asking. Always tell the reason for your question unless it's obvious from the context.

RULE 4: When You Assert Something, Say Why You Think It's So

Giving the basis for your conclusion greatly increases its credibility. Some people are more skeptical than others about any information they get. They're quick to feel that the other person doesn't know what he's talking about, or are suspicious that he has some ulterior motive for what he's saying. But even those who are most trusting feel reassured if you give the evidence.

Paul asks Susan if she knows of a good car-repair place in the neighborhood. Susan replies, "Yes, Joe's Garage. They do a good job." Can Paul feel comfortable acting on this information, or does it just raise a lot of other questions in his mind, such as: Did Susan use them only once, or a number of times? Did she use them for a simple, routine job or for a complex repair? When she says they do a good job, does that evaluation include price? speed? competence? courtesy? Has she used any other repair service in the neighborhood?

Susan would have come through as more helpful and interesting to talk to if she had said something like, "Yes, Joe's

Garage. They're really good. I've used them for some pretty tricky repair jobs over the last few years, and they've always come up with the right answer. And their price is reasonable, too. It's not low, but it's no higher than the couple of other places I've tried. And the service is a lot better."

Requiring yourself to give the evidence has another great advantage: It prods you to consider whether you're asserting something carelessly. Often people say something without having much basis for it. How often does the soundness of the information you get about an organization depend on whom you speak to in that organization? As soon as you get caught giving wrong information, people stop depending on you as a source of information, and your value goes down.

We all have to guard against our own tendency to give information without being sure. We often have the feeling that we know something better than we really do, or are surer that something's true than we should be. This occurs because when we have partial knowledge of something we fill in the rest with what seems to make sense. We then feel that we have complete understanding of the subject. We forget about the difference between what we know for a fact and what seems to make sense.

Anticipate the Evidence You'll Need Through Associative Thinking

To persuade, you need evidence. You don't know for sure what evidence you'll need because you don't know what points the other person will raise.

You'll lose far more of your persuasive impact for each point you can't handle than you'll gain for each one you can. That's because just one broken link in the reasoning chain can take away the support of all the good links. Even if your case doesn't collapse, it can weaken to the point where accepting it becomes too risky because now other links are suspect.

A good way to figure out what evidence you'll need is to anticipate objections and questions. But trying to list all of these one after the other is not the most effective way. The mind doesn't think of as many things when just listing as it does when thinking by associating. It's much more effective to hold a rehearsal dialogue with a friend where you try to sell him your idea, or to hold an imaginary dialogue with yourself where you take both roles: your role as persuader and that of the person you're persuading. In the dialogue, more points come up than you could think of by listing.

You can think of many more ideas by allowing one idea to lead to another than you can by trying to think of them all in advance. When you've brought up as many points as you can this way, you can figure out what evidence you'll need to handle them successfully.

Having Evidence Shows You've Done Your Homework

Others' skepticism goes beyond their wondering whether your facts justify your conclusion. They're concerned that you don't have any facts at all, that you're thinking off the top of your head, or wishfully.

It isn't just a question of whether your reasoning is correct, but of whether you've really done any reasoning. People can be amazingly careless about how they form their conclusions and sound off on any topic with only a few fragments of information dimly related to the topic.

Therefore, when you present an idea, the question in others' minds is, how careful were you in arriving at that idea? Even if they know you well, they feel better hearing the evidence. If someone asks them why they bought your idea, they can pass along your reasoning.

When you provide a basis, they know you've thought about

the idea, analyzed it, considered whether it makes sense. You didn't just think the whole thing up based on a lot of assumptions. You've reassured the people you're selling to; you've allayed their skepticism. Now they can look into your reasoning to see if your idea holds up.

You don't have to do a research project for every piece of evidence. In going after information, you have to weigh its persuasive value and the potential worth of the idea against the cost of getting the facts. Evidence that's suggestive rather than conclusive may cost much less and still contribute a lot of persuasive impact. Often, a phone call about someone else's experience with a similiar idea can provide convincing information.

Evaluating Cost-Effectiveness

Others will buy your idea only if they see that the benefit outweighs the cost by enough to justify the risk. The first thing they'll feel is the risk. The resistance that generally rises up in someone when he is asked to invest in an idea makes him exaggerate the risk. So you have to make the most of your benefits, and work out the cost accurately, just to get him to listen.

When you start your discussion, the best you can hope for is to set up a conflict within the other person between, on the one hand, his looking for some basis for rejecting your idea right off and, on the other, his wanting to hear more because it sounds as if you've got something and he doesn't want to risk losing it.

The reason why this conflict is the normal way to start is that resistance is the natural response to cost and risk. Much of this resistance is generalized to all ideas that call for a decision, and has little to do with the idea you're trying to sell.

To set up this conflict, you need a favorable cost-benefit balance for your idea. You have to either quantify the cost and benefit, or it has to be self-evident that the benefit outweighs the cost.

A common reaction I get to this is that you can't quantify everything. Maybe not, but you can quantify a lot more than seems possible at first. One way to quantify the difficult-to-quantify is to get the numbers from past similar ideas that have been tried.

Another way, when you can't calculate directly how much you'll gain, is to figure out how much gain you'd need to justify the investment in your idea. The smaller the gain needed, the greater the chance that you'll make it. Your needing only a small gain is a persuasive argument for your idea. After all, if you need only a one-percent gain to get a sufficient return on your investment, and you might reasonably get as much as five or even ten percent, you're likely to make the other person eager to know more.

Preparing Yourself Psychologically

Trying to sell your idea is stressful. And stress results in your tightening up. Your muscles contract. You feel tense. And this tension works against you, lowering your effectiveness as a persuader. For this tension was meant to strengthen a fight-or-flight reaction, not an interchange of ideas.

Sports psychologists are now finding that relaxing improves an athlete's performance. This is contrary to the earlier view that athletes need the tension, the flow of adrenalin. An experimental shot of adrenalin actually impaired performance. An athlete needs to relax to bring about the fine coordination of muscle and brain, the superb control, that marks superior achievement.

There are particular stress points in persuading others. These occur when the other person resists. Whenever he raises an objection, the hairs on your neck seem to rise. You become tense. You're ready to attack or run. This tension disrupts your reasoning and blocks your responsiveness to what he's saying. Instead of exercising the fine self-control and sensitive reasonableness needed to win him over, you attack with arguments and make him your opponent.

Just before you start your discussion, try to relax completely. Close your eyes and concentrate on your breathing for about a minute. Mentally, lean back in your chair, put your feet up on the desk, clasp your hands behind your head, and smile.

Then repeat to yourself six times, "I will not be an adversary." Each time you say it, put the accent on a different word. This will keep you from saying it mechanically. Never think of those you're trying to persuade as competitors. Think of them as teammates. Together, you're trying to make a decision about whether to buy your idea.

Take the position that your own final decision is not yet formed. Your idea looks good to you, but you have to hear the other person's evidence before you can decide definitely. Maybe he has sound reasoning against your idea. You certainly want to hear it so that you can make a wise decision.

You'll find that giving credit to whatever is true in the other person's objection, and then inquiring in a reasonable way about whatever seems questionable to you in it, will help keep you relaxed.

If you maintain the attitude of trying to make the right decision, even if it goes against your idea, you'll avoid the worst mistake you can make—becoming an adversary, which will make you tense. The adversary stance has probably killed enough good ideas to hold back thousands of careers, lose billions of dollars, and deprived society of countless life-enriching opportunities.

For when you become an adversary, you make the other person react like one, too, and adversaries don't listen to each other. They're each too busy thinking of what they're going to say next that will knock out the other side.

And adversaries don't think objectively about each other. They don't inquire into each other's reasoning to see if the other perhaps has done some good thinking. They don't try to learn from one another. They are closed to each other. You can't sell an idea to someone who's closed.

It's much easier to say that you won't become an adversary than it is to carry it out. When others resist, the impulse to push against them is almost overwhelming.

You'll find yourself automatically sliding into the role of an adversary, and defeating yourself. It's a hormonally caused reaction, going back tens of thousands of years. When two cavemen simultaneously came upon a potential meal and both claimed it, they didn't sit around exploring the reasoning behind each other's claims. They either argued with clubs, or one ran away. Now, you argue with words, passion, and logic, or you withdraw out of fear of offending or from a sense of hopelessness.

But to sell your ideas you've got to psych yourself beforehand. You've got to stay on a course of reasonably examining the other person's position and comparing it with yours, and encouraging the other person to do the same. You've got to watch yourself carefully to resist the impulse either to pound away with words or to withdraw without making your case. It takes a high degree of self-discipline and relaxation to avoid becoming an adversary, and instead to inquire into the other person's resistance. But the tremendous gain resulting makes it worth doing. In this book, you'll find highly effective techniques for dealing constructively with the other person's resistance.

‖ 2 ‖ Why We Misunderstand Each Other

The Strong Urge to Jump to Conclusions

As soon as you start talking to someone she's mentally poised to grasp your point. If she can't see what you're getting at, she can become edgy. She doesn't know where you're taking her. She's craving to understand, and you're frustrating her.

You don't mean to annoy her. Your heart's in the right place. You want to give her the background, show her the problem before you tell her your idea. Then when you come to the idea, she'll appreciate the good sense in it.

You're anxious that if you tell the idea right off, she'll turn it down before you can explain the gain. And you want to save her from losing out on a brilliant idea, which she'll thank you for later.

The trouble is, we all want to understand now, see the whole. When we start to receive information, we immediately try to make sense of it. We're uncomfortable until the parts fall into place.

Some of us are more uncomfortable than others about not seeing the connections. It's like an itch that won't go away. To scratch the itch we invent some connections. We think, This is what he must mean, and we let down and listen less. Often, we react to our invention as though it were the other person's idea, and we reject his idea based on the conclusion we jumped to rather than on what he's really getting to.

To varying degrees, we all find it hard to tolerate ambiguity, to be uncertain of what it's all about. There are even psychological tests to measure people's intolerance of ambiguity. People with high intolerance form the picture with very little information. So, very often they get it wrong. If they have more tolerance, they wait to learn more.

Ironically, the less people can stand the uncertainty of not knowing, the more opinionated they are. They have an answer for everything. They can tell you what's causing a recession, what to do about crime in the streets, why the kids aren't learning in school, whether the suspect in a front-page crime is guilty, and what women and men really want from each other.

We all jump to conclusions on scanty information. One day I called the police before my wife and I entered our house because a screen door I thought I had left open was now locked. I figured that maybe there was a burglar inside who had locked the door to prevent being surprised by someone's entering.

I followed the policeman up the stairs to the master bedroom, where he immediately proclaimed that I'd been burgled. He pointed to the evidence: the contents of a woman's purse spread out all over the bed. He sensibly figured that the burglar had emptied the purse in searching for cash.

With a mixture of relief and embarrassment, I explained that my wife always emptied a purse on the bed when she wanted to use it but didn't want its contents at the moment. She then left the contents there until bedtime.

We all jump to conclusions often. Someone has a surly look on his face and we think he's angry at us. After examining us, the doctor asks if we ever have shortness of breath or dizziness, and we think, What did she find wrong? Yet these may be routine questions that are part of the examination. We get angry at a storekeeper who refuses to cash our check. We resent not being given that little bit of service. We don't consider that the policy was adopted because there had been so many bad checks.

A business person told me that she felt hurt when she overheard a false remark that the reason she donated some merchandise to charity was because she couldn't sell it. When people don't know your motivations, they'll guess at them.

Start at the End

"So what's the bottom line?" Whether he asks you or not, the other person always wants to know it. Since you only irritate him when you keep him waiting for it, tell it to him right off. Don't be afraid of a no. It's not the end. You can always ask why.

We're all bottom-line creatures. We want to know right off what it comes down to. If the other person doesn't tell us quickly enough, we figure something out for ourselves, and react to that. Whether it's right or wrong, it's better than not knowing.

You keep chasing big and little bottom lines all your life. You ask yourself: Will this idea work? Will I enjoy my vacation? Does my mate really love me? Will I get a raise? Am I going to get well? Will this risk pay off? How do I compare with the others? Will I make it big? Will I fail?

You keep looking for information that gives you bottom-line answers. The trouble is, there's never enough information to be sure of the answers. It's like looking at jigsaw-puzzle pictures with parts missing. There often are parts missing.

Is this a good time to see the boss about my idea? It's before lunch and she might be hungry. But if she doesn't enjoy her lunch, she might be irritable afterward. She seems to be greeting me in a friendly fashion but her smile is a little more fleeting than usual. Is it because of me or something else? She only nods as I explain my idea. Does this mean she understands it, or is she uninterested? She says she wants to think about it some more. Is this really so, or is it her polite way of rejecting the idea?

All the uncertainties are too much to take. We can't wait for the answers because we need to know how to react. So we fill in the answers based on our past experience, prejudices, wishes, and gut feelings.

Listen to this conversation:

"Hey, Tom, remember that shipment to Universal?"

"Yeah. What about it?"

"Well, they claim it wasn't what they ordered."

"What are they talking about? I personally followed that order all the way through to make sure it met their specifications. I know what went in their order. That's a big account, and I want to make sure we keep it. So don't tell me the package we made up for them contained the wrong material."

"It didn't. I'm only telling you what they said because I know how concerned you are to keep them happy."

"Well, they must have used it wrong. One of their people probably screwed up, and they're blaming us."

"No, they didn't screw up. They did get the wrong stuff, and they're hopping mad. Said it nearly cost them a day's production. The trucker dropped off some stuff that was supposed to go to a different customer."

"What! Get the trucker on the phone."

"Hold on. It wasn't the trucker's fault. One of our people in shipping gave the trucker the wrong package. What I'm getting at is that we better take a look at what's going on in shipping because this happened a couple of times before. We better change the system or maybe the clerk."

"Why the hell didn't you say so in the first place instead of driving up my blood pressure?"

Start at the end and then go back and tell how you got there. If you do this, you'll stop the other person from jumping to the wrong conclusion and then reacting negatively.

Tuning Out

People are constantly tuning out. It's hard to believe this as they gaze at us with steady, quiet faces, nod their heads seriously, and say uh-huh agreeably. You'd be flabbergasted if you could see their minds darting this way and that like pinballs bouncing off the barriers they bump against.

The mind is very restless. It can't stand still. It intermittently moves from its point of focus to some other thought, and then returns.

In the second or two that it's away, it loses a word or two. That missing word is a larger information gap than you'd think. A psychological experiment shows that when one word is missing from a twelve-word sentence, the chance of inferring that word from the other eleven words is only fifty percent. And the chance of inferring just the meaning of that word without getting the exact word is only seventy-five percent.

Tuning out for only a second or two every ten seconds or so is the most attentive a person can be. Much of the time we tune out for longer—five, or ten, or thirty seconds or more—depending on the tug of other problems and how much the present discussion interests us. The longer the tune-out, the greater the chance of error in filling the gap.

This tuning out gives you less trouble in a discussion than it does in a twelve-word sentence since a discussion has a context and much repetition. Still, the gaps develop, and we often fill them based on what came before and after the gap. When there's more than one way to fill that gap, we often get it wrong.

Since tuning out is a fact of life, and there's nothing you

can do to prevent either the other person's tuning out or your own, you've got to make sure that each of you has gotten the other's thinking right. You can do this by giving and getting feedback, and by repeating.

We have to make sure on a routine basis because we're not aware that we're filling in gaps with our imagination. We do it so quickly that we don't see that those gaps could have been filled in other ways and still match up logically with what went before and what comes after.

We're always forming pictures in our minds from the words that come at us. But the words don't contain all the details; a picture does. Later, we remember the pictures we formed and we act on and tell others these details as though we heard them rather than imagined them.

The police encounter this continually in the different stories witnesses tell after observing the same crime. Descriptions of the robber's height, weight, age, dress, coloring, what he said, and of the getaway car vary all over the lot. While all the action was happening, the witnesses' jumpy minds tuned out intermittently, causing information gaps. Then, without realizing it, they used their imaginations to fill in the gaps because gaps make them nervous.

High motivation to get the information reduces tuning out, but doesn't eliminate it. There is always an irreducible minimum simply because the mind won't stand still.

This should reassure those of you who are afraid that you tune out too much. Stop worrying. Everyone else is tuning out also. It should also make you less irritated with someone you catch tuning out on you. He couldn't help it. Just remember your own tuning out.

How often have you tuned out and missed a person's name just at the moment he's introduced to you? So you tell him you didn't catch his name and ask him to please tell you again. He tells you again and you miss it again. You can't ask him again because he might start edging away from you.

Guard Your Credibility

How can you sell an idea if no one believes you? No matter how brilliant your idea is, people figure that there's something wrong with it. They don't trust your facts. Yet often people lie or shade the truth. They don't realize what they're risking.

Given enough stress, many people do worse things than they ever dreamed they were capable of. Some people amaze themselves by ignoring the cries for help of someone being killed; or steal when they're broke; or falsify scientific data; or invent a news story they present as true. All of us have read about such cases.

Isn't it likely then that many more of us would just stretch the truth, misrepresent things a bit, if we want something badly enough? The same thing stresses each of us differently. We try to remove the stress. When this leads us to lie, we can pay a tremendous price in the long run.

Lying isn't cost-effective. The risk is too great. If you're caught, you lose credibility. Considering the short-run gain and the risk, the price is way too high.

The same holds true if you pass along false information. If you don't tell its source, you become responsible for it. When someone learns it's false, you lose credibility.

Now consider this. If you're right half the time and wrong half the time, is your credibility fifty percent? No, it's not. It's practically zero. Any information you give is useless since no one would dare to use it with the risk at fifty percent. This means that you're isolated. You can't communicate.

How hard is it to get your credibility back? Plenty hard. If people don't use your information, how will they ever know if it's true? They won't, which is why it's so hard to raise your credibility. You can do it slowly by giving evidence for your information, and by showing them that it was right although they didn't use it. Bit by bit they'll gain confidence and start to try it. As they experience success with it your credibility will come back.

How Disagreement Reduces Listening

When two people disagree, they don't listen much to each other. Each is thinking of arguments to convince the other, rather than exploring the other's thinking to find the reason for the disagreement. When you disagree, you should be listening the most and inquiring into the other person's thinking. Even if he gives you a reason, often he doesn't give you the full reason, or doesn't tell you what he bases his reason on.

When we disagree we tend to fill in gaps from our imagination because we're not willing to wait for the information. We're not in the mood to wait because disagreement stresses us. Our first priority is to remove the stress by eliminating the disagreement. But eliminating it by giving way is also stressful. This leaves us feeling we need to win the argument as quickly as we can, so we jump to conclusions about the basis of the other person's reasoning.

The lowered listening is a form of resistance arising out of the need to win. It's a defensive move. If we don't listen, we can't be convinced. Also, we feel sure we're right, so why waste the effort absorbing something that's wrong?

Listen to the following conversation:

"You've got to take either Helen or me off this project. We just don't work well together. Every time I suggest something, she disagrees. We spend more time arguing than working."

"Helen and you are perfect for this project. You complement

each other just right in technical knowledge. Each of you knows what the other doesn't."

"We don't hit it off. We rub each other the wrong way. Helen is stubborn. If it's not her idea, she doesn't want to hear it. We're just not making any progress."

"People have to compromise. You've got to listen to each other, talk things over. You can't always have it your way and neither can she. You've got to do what's right for the project."

"Some people just won't listen. They don't try to get along. They're too sensitive. They can't take any criticism. They blow up too easily. That's Helen. It's too hard working with her. I can take it if I have to, but it's not good for the project."

"Look, when you were a kid, you played on a ball team, right? You didn't like some of the people on the team but you played anyway. You didn't quit the game. And often your team won, right? So get in there and play to win. And if you have any more problems, my door is always open."

If they had listened thoughtfully to each other, it could have gone like this, because listening means asking questions to fill in the gaps:

"You've got to take either Helen or me off this project. We just don't work well together. Every time I suggest something, she disagrees. We spend more time arguing than working."

"Arguing a lot is upsetting and can really set the project back. What do you argue about? Maybe I can think of something. The two of you have just the right blend of technical knowledge. You each know things the other doesn't."

"We argue about everything. She just doesn't listen. Like yesterday. I suggested we buy some equipment to do some tests that we're going to have to do every so often. Helen said the equipment is too costly and that we should give it out to a lab to do whenever we need the tests. I felt that's too costly, and we got into a big fight about it."

"Well, it is worthwhile to consider buying equipment you

might have to use a lot. How many times would you have to use it to make it worth buying?"

"It worked out to about fifty times. Where we got hung up was on how many times we would have to run the test. That depends on how many tests you have to run before you get the answer. Helen claimed it would be much less than fifty, and I felt it would probably be much more. We ended up shouting at each other."

"It could be hard to pin down exactly. Was there some way you could have used to work out the probabilities of finding the answer at different amounts of testing? Like estimating how many tests it would take to check out the most likely answers, or maybe finding out what other people had done, which might have reduced the amount of testing?"

"We didn't get that far. We were too angry, so we dropped it for the time being."

"What was the anger all about?"

"I felt that she wasn't really listening to my side. She just wanted her own way. And we had to make a decision that was economical."

"Why do you suppose she was so angry?"

"I don't know. Probably because I wouldn't give in to her, so she couldn't get what she wanted."

"Looking at it as though you were a third party, would you say that you have any more evidence for your position than she has for hers?"

"No, not really. I see what you're getting at. She could be angry at me for the same reason I'm angry at her. We're just butting heads instead of trying to figure out together which way to go."

Listening while disagreeing is difficult. Our bodies are charged up to fight. To listen, we need to mentally massage ourselves into a relaxed state and decide that we care more about finding out the truth than about winning.

Motivation Loss

Early in your discussion, after you first mention your idea, the other person's motivation may start to slide. As soon as he knows what you want and the benefit he is to gain, he thinks of problems with it.

Your idea disturbs his equilibrium. He was adjusted to things as they are. Suddenly, you introduce risk, which generally accompanies any kind of investment. At the same time, you promise gain. This makes for conflict within him, which makes him want to mentally withdraw.

Besides, he has quickly filled in the information gaps by using his imagination. He already has a mental picture of your idea, so he thinks your explaining further is superfluous. He doesn't consider that his picture may be wrong. He just loses interest in listening further.

To hold his interest, you have to keep your remarks brief and involve him by asking questions. Watch that you don't repeat too much or overexplain. As you go through the discussion, let him lead the way with his questions and objections.

There is a common illusion that the one doing the talking has control of the conversation. Actually, the only thing we control while talking is who's sounding off at the moment. The other person can be tuning out.

Because of this illusion, we are often reluctant to ask a question. It means giving away the talking role. But asking a question is far more controlling than is explaining. Our question requests the other person to develop information that matches the contour of our question. That's why asking a question requires assertiveness. We should do it gently, and tell why we're asking.

When we explain, he can tune out, which is not readily noticeable. When we ask a question, although he can evade, doing so is quite apparent and costs him some discomfort. He knows that his evading suggests something negative.

Talk about the particular aspect he brings up as the discussion proceeds. His motivation to listen is highest toward the topic he raises at any point.

Don't preset your discussion when you're talking one to one. Make each of your remarks fit what he has just brought up. However, you have to prearrange your topics when you present to a group.

Watch Out for Ambiguity

It's amazing how often ambiguity occurs. It occurs because there's an information gap, which makes your meaning unclear. The trouble is, the other person often fills in the gap from her imagination without even realizing that she's doing so. Her understanding of what you mean then depends on what she put in the gap.

At the same time, you don't see the gap because it seems to you that what you have in mind is the only thing that fits what you said. If what she inserted in the gap and what you have in mind are different, there could be a misunderstanding about your whole idea.

Information gaps are common not only because people tune out so much but also because of what words are like. Each word stands for a kind of thing, but never for a specific one of that kind of thing. *Dog* stands for all dogs and not for any particular dog. *Lamp* covers all kinds of lamps. The more abstract words such as *justice* and *love* are even more vague.

Adjectives such as *complicated* and *safe* are also very general since they can be applied to all kinds of things and situations. Furthermore, how complicated is *complicated*, and how safe is *safe*?

To get specific, we have to add more words to narrow down what we're saying to the specific idea in our mind. We narrow down *house* by adding that it's a white stucco two-story house with a large lawn in front of it and a patio in the back. Each word we add narrows *house* down further to a specific house we have in mind.

When someone talks to us, we form mental pictures from his words. Pictures are completely specific. They don't show just kinds of things. They show the particular things.

When you're selling an idea, you're picturing in your own mind the specifics of your idea. Since you use words when you tell it to the other person, you're talking about kinds of things. You try to narrow down the kinds of things to the specific things, by adding more words. At the same time, the other person is trying to reconstruct in his mind, from your words, a mental picture that looks the same as yours.

Whenever you leave out some information, a gap occurs in his picture of your idea because you haven't narrowed down what you're saying, to your specific idea. What you're saying could also cover variations of your idea. The other person fills in the gap with an assumption that he makes so naturally and quickly that he doesn't see the other possible variations. The variation of your idea that he formed may be worse than the one you mean, and he turns off on what he thinks is your idea. So be as specific as you can.

The reason you leave information gaps without realizing it is because you form mental pictures. In your mental picture, everything is filled in. When you tell your idea while looking inward at your mental picture of it, it seems to you that there are no gaps in what you're saying since there are no gaps in your picture.

You don't realize that your words are generalities that need more and more narrowing down in order to match just the relevant parts of your picture. You can never match the whole picture because pictures require you to visualize much more than is relevant to the idea. You have to decide just how much you have to tell, and often you fall on the low side.

Listen to this:

HE: Let's have a party soon. We owe some people anyway, and I'd like to get together with some others we have fun with. But let's keep it low-cost.

SHE: I think we ought to put it off for a while. We had one not too long ago. It's a lot of work. Maybe I'm negative about it because I just feel tired at the moment.

HE: Listen, we don't have to make it complicated, and we can keep it small.

At this point, she's picturing a sit-down dinner with twelve guests. To economize, she'll make a chicken- rather than veal-in-wine-sauce dish with rice and salad, and domestic wine, and a rich pastry for dessert. He's picturing a serve-yourself meal for eight guests with spaghetti and hero sandwiches and beer.

SHE: Well, okay. If you don't think it's too much work.

HE: No, there's nothing to it.

She's thinking of his doing the shopping, some of the cooking, the preparing of the salad and dressing, the setting of the table, and the cleaning up afterward, while she does the planning, the calling, and the rest of the cooking. He's thinking of running out and buying some takeout items and throwing out the paper plates afterward.

SHE: Whom should we invite?

HE: Oh, some close friends and a few people we owe.

They each have different people in mind as well as some of the same people.

SHE: Well, maybe you're right.

HE: Let's not wait too long.

She's thinking of six weeks away, and he's thinking of three.

He doesn't realize that the idea she bought is quite different from the one he tried to sell her. Because of our quickness to assume that our words are conveying our pictured idea completely, we leave gaps without realizing it. Therefore, we need to get feedback from the other person on what his understanding is.

Attributing Motivations to Others

When we don't know why someone is doing something, we fill in the why from our imagination. A person's motivation for his action intrigues us. When we don't know it, we fill in the gap by assuming what it is. This affects what we make of the information he gives us.

When you're selling an idea, always tell why you want to do what you're suggesting. Otherwise, the other person might figure you've got something to gain personally that you're hiding.

If a supervisor suggests hiring another person for the unit, and doesn't give a good reason, the other person might feel that the supervisor is trying to enlarge his little empire, or wants to do less work. If a wife suggests accompanying her husband on a clothes-shopping trip and doesn't explain why, he might wonder if she disliked what he bought last time, or if she's afraid he'll buy something that doesn't fit well.

Whenever you suggest something, tell why you want to do it. Make sure your reasons soundly justify your suggestions. Otherwise, there's going to be a lot of speculation about your motivations.

|| 3 || Getting the Other Person to Listen

Arousing the Desire to Know More

It costs a person time and effort to listen to and evaluate the idea you're trying to sell him. He has to concentrate on what you're saying, which means fighting off his inner thoughts and feelings that are all competing for his attention. And he has to relate your presentation to his experience in order to develop a useful picture of what you're saying.

On top of all that, he has to be patient. He has to wait for you to build your idea, since you can only say one word at a time. While his mind can absorb information much more quickly, he has to control the urge to shout, Faster, faster, faster.

If we could only talk in pictures instead of words, he'd see it all immediately, and there'd be no misunderstandings from information gaps. Maybe that will come at some future stage in evolution. We'll send an idea through mind waves, and the other person will see the picture and receive in silence the sounds, smells, and feelings that are part of the idea.

Also, before he even starts listening, he worries a little that you'll present an idea that would cost him something and then won't pay off; and that it would mean change, which is uncomfortable. But he meets with you anyway, because he doesn't want to make you feel bad; and because you just might have a good idea.

Since the other person's listening costs him time, concentration, thought, patience, and worry in anticipation of risk and change, you'd better make sure that you've got something worth listening to, and that you make the listening interesting and your remarks easy to grasp. If you don't, it will be harder to get him to listen the next time.

If you keep him waiting to find out whether the cost of listening is going to pay off, he'll become irritated. He needs to be able to think right away, Hey, this is worth exploring. I've got to find out more.

Right off, tell him what you want, and what he's going to gain. Some of you may be thinking, I can't do that. As soon as he hears what I want and what it costs, he'll turn me down. If I don't explain the background before I ask for what I want, he won't appreciate why he should buy the idea.

But why should he listen to the background if he doesn't even know what you want and what he'll gain? You can't make your whole presentation in your opening remark. You first have to arouse his interest, sell him on listening.

Suppose you start by telling him that he'll get twenty back on the ten he spends if he does what you suggest. Won't he want to know more? His reaction might be, How would I get back twenty by doing that? He might be skeptical, but he'll want to check it out to make sure he isn't missing something good.

The Bottom-Line Opening

The bottom line is the most motivating part of your whole idea. Start with it because the first two minutes of your discussion are critical. That's when the other person decides whether to look further or to drop the idea.

The bottom line is the end point of your thinking. You've worked out what you want done, what it will cost, and what the return will be, why you think you'll get it, the problems and risks, and how you'll deal with them. Now, start at the end. The rest of the discussion will then become an examining together of how you got there and whether your bottom line is justified.

Suppose Anne wants to get Jim to come to the point more directly in his conversations. Jim talks too much about what he's going to say before he ever says it. Anne would be making the same mistake if she said the following:

> Jim, you have a tendency to talk a little too much before you get to your point. You lead up to it and the other person doesn't know where you're going. It makes him impatient and he's likely to find it harder to follow you. I know that you feel you're trying to give him some background so that he'll understand your point better. But it's actually harder for him to follow you. He might even listen less closely and then miss the significance of what you're saying. And he might tend to avoid having discussions with you. But if you'd come right to the point more, people would listen better and absorb more of your ideas. And they'll be more interested in talking with you. As a result, you'll sell a lot more of your ideas.

The bottom line is that Jim will sell a lot more of his ideas. This has the most persuasive impact.

Since your first objective is to sell the other person on listening, why not begin with the part that has the most persuasive force—the end point in your thinking? Then follow with any explanation that's needed.

Using a bottom-line opening, Anne could have said:

Jim, as a suggestion for talking more effectively, you'd sell a lot more of your ideas if you'd start with the bottom line instead of leading up to it. People get impatient and annoyed when they have to wait to see the point, and they don't want to listen.

Quantifying the Bottom Line

Quantifying the bottom line motivates listening far more. Quantify it whenever you can. In many cases it's just a matter of doing some calculations. In other cases, you have to use some imagination. You can use estimates and probabilities.

When you find yourself thinking, You can't quantify that, try again to find a way. It's worth the effort. When the other person hears a number, he figures you've done your homework. Maybe you've done some interesting research to get that number. He wonders how you arrived at it. He feels that since you have a number, the whole idea didn't just come off the top of your head.

Take the example above. It seems at first glance as though you couldn't possibly get any number for how many more ideas Jim would sell. But look at it this way. All people aren't going to get impatient and annoyed to the same extent when they have to wait until you get to your point. They'll vary all over the lot. Some will take it in stride, some will get moderately annoyed, and some will get so irritated they'll stop listening or jump to a negative conclusion about what you're getting at.

Let's make an estimate that the twenty percent most annoyed people will tune you out or jump to a negative conclusion and get turned off. This means that twenty percent more people would have listened if you had started with the bottom line. Let's be conservative and assume that only half of this twenty percent would have bought your idea.

In your bottom-line opening you could then say, "sell probably ten percent more of your ideas" instead of "sell a lot more of your ideas." Then, if he asked you where you got the ten percent, you could explain your reasoning. If he disagrees with your estimate, you can ask him for his.

Linking Thinking

It's easy for people in a conversation to lose touch with each other's thinking. Both people are tuning out every so often, jumping to conclusions, and leaving information gaps in what they're saying so that their meaning isn't clear. We have to make sure our thinking is linked to the other person's, so that each of us is building the same mental picture.

By repeating, you can fill in the gaps in what the other person absorbed. But you have to be careful about repeating. It's double-edged. If you just say again what you said before, you'll annoy the other person and drive him to tune out. Not only will you sound dull, but the other person will think you consider him dense.

One good way to repeat so nobody notices you're doing it is to repeat what you said before in place of saying words that stand for it. Instead of asking, What do you think of that idea? say, What do you think of hiring another person? if that was the idea you had proposed.

Other ways of repeating that keep the other person listening are: giving examples, asking questions about the idea, using audiovisuals, and summarizing.

Another way to link thinking is for each of you to compare his understanding with what the other person intended. If the other person doesn't give or ask for feedback, you'll have to ask questions in both directions. Is this what you mean? and then explain your understanding; and, Is what I'm saying clear to you?

A more precise way to use the question to check understanding is to ask whether you're right in expecting a certain thing to follow from what the other person is saying; or whether he understands that a certain thing results from what you're saying. The questions below show this:

"This is a very important affair we're going to, and the impression we make will mean a lot. Try to look your very best."
"Should I buy a new outfit?"

"Things are tight but we have to have that machine. Get the lowest priced model that has the features we need."
"Does this mean that I shouldn't take into account how long it lasts and how often it's likely to need repair?"

"I need your help on this project to get it finished on time."
"I'll be glad to work with you on it, but do you realize this means I'll have to get some help with my work in order to keep things going?"

"I'll have to lose twenty pounds to get into this dress, but I'm going to buy it anyway. It looks great, and I've got a month to take off the weight. Then I can dazzle them at the Christmas party."
"I can understand your wanting to wear that dress for the Christmas party. But do you realize that to lose twenty pounds in a month, you'd practically have to not eat at all?"

The Risk in Not Risking

Whenever you propose a good idea to someone, you put him in a bind. He has a chance to lose whether or not he buys your idea. If he buys it, there's always the chance that it won't turn out the way you expect, and he'll lose his investment. And if he doesn't buy it, he risks losing what he might have gained.

Once you've told him your idea, he can't go back to the way things were before. Now he has to take responsibility for a decision that can have as much consequence one way as the other. No wonder he's reluctant to listen. He's afraid you might have a really good idea.

As he listens, part of him is hoping that you'll say something that enables him to reasonably reject your idea. Then he won't have to worry about losing his investment, and he won't have to be anxious that maybe he lost out on a good thing.

Let's listen to how the conversation might sound if a manager were to say what was really on his mind as an employee tries to sell him an idea.

EMPLOYEE: I've got an idea for how we can save $25,000 a year in production costs for a one-time investment of $50,000. How's that for a payback?

MANAGER: It's too risky.

EMPLOYEE: How do you mean it's too risky? I haven't told you the idea yet.

MANAGER: Any risk is too much. I like an idea with no risk at all. Is this one of those?

EMPLOYEE: Well, no. There's always some risk with any idea. But the payoff for this idea easily justifies the risk. Wait'll you hear it.

MANAGER: Well, then, can I count on there being something really wrong with your idea so that at least I can turn it down?

EMPLOYEE: Turn it down? Why would you want to turn down my idea? I'm conscientious, competent, loyal, and get along with people.

MANAGER: No, no, it's got nothing to do with you personally. I think well of your performance except when you threaten me with a good idea. I just don't want to risk turning down an idea that might have worked.

EMPLOYEE: And you also don't want to invest in a good idea.

MANAGER: That's right. Not as long as there's any risk. I think you've got the picture.

EMPLOYEE: Well, listen, to tell you the truth, I am a little uneasy about this idea. I can see holes in it. I just didn't want to face them.

MANAGER: Now you interest me. Why don't we talk about your idea? But those holes better be too big to plug. You don't want to lose your credibility.

Is it any wonder that you encounter resistance when you try to sell your good ideas?

People generally exaggerate the risk when they're making a decision. For there's more at stake than the investment. They're also risking both their self-image and their image to others as a smart decision maker. And the risk is still greater for those who find the pain of losing greater than the pleasure in winning.

To get the other person to view the risk realistically, remind him of the potential loss in not risking. This could mean losing the benefits of your idea. Considering the evidence you've presented, you might ask, Which way is the risk greater: taking my idea or leaving it? This might neutralize both the image and pain-of-losing factors, since both of these would come into play if he loses out by not taking your idea.

Holding Attention.

A big mistake we often make is that we think the other person is listening as long as she's sitting quietly. We've got so much we want to say that we can't resist what seems like a good chance to get it all in. It's frustrating to be interrupted by the other person's remarks. They keep stopping us from developing a complete picture of our idea in all its beauty.

Since it's irritating to get interrupted in anything we do, we don't see the gain for us in the other person's interrupting remark. Actually, she's telling us she has to stop listening for the moment, so we might as well stop talking. It may be that she first has to absorb what we've told her so that her mind is clear to receive more. She might also want to say something at that point, which distracts her from listening further.

Many people seem to think that if you want to get an idea across, you just tell it in a clear, interesting way. The more concerned they are about selling the idea, the more they polish what they intend to say.

When they think this way, they're considering only the problem of how to make it interesting. They're assuming that people listen to what's said as long as it sounds good. The reality is that people can only listen so long. For as you talk, what you say brings up in the other person's mind all kinds of related thoughts and feelings.

The other person thinks of other ideas similar to yours; of what happened in the past; and about how your idea could be used and its effects on others. He worries that he might be missing some hole in your idea, and feels anxious when he thinks that your idea might fail.

As you talk, associated ideas keep coming up within him, and he needs to talk about how your idea affects him. This need distracts him from listening further. Each remark you make generates in him thoughts and feelings that dam up his receiving channel. No more can pass through his mind until he discharges by talking.

To keep him in touch with your thinking, you have to find out his concerns and respond to them. Ask questions about his reactions to what you're saying, or at least pause to encourage him to talk. Then comment on his remark. As you talk to him, put yourself in his place and try to imagine at what point you would feel that you've listened enough if you were he. That's the point to ask him to comment. It's likely to be after twenty to forty seconds of talking. Then link up with his comment by remarking on how it relates to your idea.

Making the Conversation Attractive

Think of the conversation as a place. This place exists only as long as your conversation lasts, but for the moment it's the thought-feeling environment for you and the other person. You're both in it, being affected by it, reacting to it.

No matter what the topic is, the thought-feeling environment can be irritating or soothing, dull or stimulating, depressing or inspiring. You have the power to design it. Even when the other person is dragging it down, you can give it a lift. Making this environment satisfying to him helps sell your idea.

How can you make the thought-feeling environment as pleasant as possible? For one thing, you can make the other person feel good about himself. Compliment him on any sound reasoning, useful facts, and entertaining comments he makes.

Avoid making him lose face. Don't corner him logically. Allow him to move away from his position without his having to admit he's wrong. Rather than ever telling him he's wrong, say that your information or conclusion is different from his.

Put him at ease by sharing your thinking with him. When you ask a question, tell him why that question came to your mind, and how the information you're asking him for fits into your thinking. When you tell him something, include where you got it from or what you base it on.

Share both the talking and the listening time. If you talk too much, you'll frustrate him, because he needs to talk in order to work things out, discharge his feelings, and get the pleasure of educating or entertaining. If you talk too little, you'll drain him by making him talk more than he wants to, and you'll not be contributing any knowledge or amusement.

If the other person wants more of his share of talking time, accommodate him by doing more listening if it doesn't frustrate you. Some people have a great need to talk. They can hardly control it. Often, they helplessly watch themselves going on and on as if their mouths had a life of their own. The other person senses that you're giving up your talking time and appreciates your generosity. When the other person adds little to the conversation, try adding more in order to accommodate him. At the same time, ask some questions to help him get started.

Some of you may be thinking, What about me? Why shouldn't he be accommodating me? It's not a question of what's fair, or of gaining your rights. If you relax and ask yourself, How much does it really matter? you might enjoy making him happy through your power to create an enjoyable thought-feeling environment. And you just might sell your idea.

Make Your Remarks Easy to Listen To

To make a conversation successful, you have to satisfy both your needs and the other person's. Both of you feel a need to do the following: see the point immediately; express your ideas as soon as, and in whatever form, they come to mind; tell the other person she's wrong and correct her thinking as soon as you become aware of a mistake; let out your feelings of anger, anxiety, impatience, and frustration; and express your impulses to interrupt, criticize, change the subject, dismiss a bothersome thought, and keep talking till you're tired of it.

It's not easy for you to respond equally to your needs and the other person's. You feel immediately the constant press of your own needs, while you only know as an abstract idea that the other person also has them. It takes a lot of self-discipline to attend to the other person's needs when you're continually being prodded by your own. But when you're selling your idea, it's better to give even more attention to her needs.

People commonly give way to their need to explain their idea all at once. For one thing, they're afraid of a no from the other person if she doesn't see the whole picture. What they don't realize is that they've defeated themselves by flooding the other person with more information than she can hold on to. Often, it's too much work for her to sift out what she did catch from what she didn't and to ask for what she missed. So she justs stops listening, or decides against your idea.

You'll be much more effective if you open with a brief statement of what you're asking for and the benefit that easily justifies it. The benefit is likely to motivate the other person to ask for more information. But even if she says no, you can ask why in view of the benefit. So a no can be just a starting point.

Another reason we keep talking on is because we hate to be interrupted. We have a natural drive to complete what we start. Interruption irritates us. So we keep going and irritate the other person instead. He can't hold on to what we're saying, and he can't keep still for that long.

Our wanting to discharge tension also keeps us talking. We're all geared up to sell our idea. The juices are flowing. We want to keep moving until we've won. Our attitude is: If the other person wants us to stop, let him buy our idea. But not only have we lost the other person, he's also less inclined to listen to us the next time.

Other impulses keep coming up in us. Something we've just said brings another thought to our minds. That thought seems to us related and meaningful even if it's not in the direct line of what we're saying. We're not sure anyway where the boundary of our idea is. So we say these related ideas as little asides to what we were saying, and then we add further asides to our first ones.

All ideas have other ideas related to them. And these other ideas connect with still other ideas. Every idea is part of an endless map of ideas linked to each other in various ways. We have to mentally draw the boundary around the territory of our idea, to include the related ideas that we mean to include. It's just as if we were drawing a boundary around a city to define what territory that city includes, although the land on one side of the boundary connects with the land on the other.

When we make asides within our remarks, we confuse the other person. He thinks we're going in one direction and his mind moves ahead to anticipate what we're coming to. Suddenly we turn down a side path. He wonders, Did I understand wrongly where we're heading, or is this just a momentary digression to be followed by a return to the original direction? And if we continue too far on our side path, or turn off onto still another path, he may wonder if his understanding of our idea's boundary is correct.

Another need we have that causes trouble is to tell all of our reasoning, even when parts of it are obvious to the other person. While we get the satisfaction of completing the picture, we lose out by talking down to the other person.

Suppose an employee says the following to his boss:

"We want to keep everyone happy, give them the feeling that they have lots of opportunities here, that they can get ahead. Morale is important for productivity. I think we ought to post all job openings on the bulletin board so that employees who feel they're qualified can apply. This will give them a better chance to advance and to get into jobs they like better. It will improve our relations with employees."

In the first two sentences and the last, the employee is telling the boss what she already knows. It's irritating to be told the obvious, for it implies that you don't know what you should, and what others do.

Listen to this conversation between a mother and her teenage daughter. Watch the needs of both erupt all over the place. The mother begins.

"Being responsible and self-disciplined is very important to success in living. We shouldn't make others suffer from our lack of discipline, or depend on them to take care of us as though we were babies. Look at your room, how messy it is. Look at that blouse, lying there crushed and wrinkled. That's an expensive blouse but I got it on sale, a third off, because I watch the papers for sales, which you should do, too. I want you to keep your room neat and clean so when someone comes in here they get a good impression of you. They won't think you're sloppy and careless."

"Nobody comes in here except me and my friends, and my friends—"

"I come in here and it offends me. Your father comes in here and he—"

"What do you mean, I'm irresponsible and have no discipline? Look at my grades, all A's and B's. And I'm in the school play, in student government, and on the school paper. You can't do all those things—"

"And keep your room clean, too, you're going to tell me. That's no excuse. It just takes a few minutes each day to—"

"That's not what I was going to say. If you'd stop interrupting, you'd find out. You can't do all those things if you're not—"

"Who's interrupting you? You just interrupted me. And listening without interrupting is another thing that takes self-discipline. Besides, I don't think you should be in the school play. All those rehearsals. It takes time away from studying. Your grades are going to—"

"Look, grades aren't the only thing. Extracurriculars are

important, too. There are many things to learn and experience in high school that you don't get in the classroom. I want to become well-rounded, not just—"

"You look well-rounded to me with all the fattening foods you stuff into yourself. You've got to watch your eating if—"

"Listen, Mom, I've got to go. I'm late for a meeting. Talk to you later." (She exits.)

Now let's look at how this might have gone if the mother had done a better job of accommodating for her daughter's needs in the conversation.

"The house would look a lot better to me if you would make your bed each morning and keep your room neat. It bothers me when I see all the disorder in your room. I think you'd feel better, too." (She comes right to the point and doesn't imply that her daughter is irresponsible and undisciplined.)

"Listen, Mom, it's my room, so I ought to be able to keep it the way I want. If it bothers you, just keep the door closed."

"It's true, I could keep the door closed, but don't you think the hall is darker that way, and the closed door cuts off the view from the windows and cuts down the sense of space? I hate closed doors. I like the feeling of openness."

"I see what you mean, but I just don't have time to do it. When I get up, I'm always rushing around and just about make it to school on time."

"I know you're in a hurry in the morning and it's hard to think of doing anything that slows you down. How long do you think it would take you to make your bed? I'm thinking that if you put everything away the night before and prepared what you're going to wear the next morning, all you'd have to do is make your bed. How long do you think that would take?"

"I could do that in about three minutes, but I can't even fit that in. If you're three minutes late for school—or even one minute—you're late."

"Of course, you can't be late for school. What if you get up three minutes earlier? You would hardly feel that."

"Oh, Mom, I'm often up late the night before, doing my homework, and I've got the school play and student government. I like to sleep as long as I can in the morning and not worry about having to do something then."

"I know you work hard and have a lot to do, and I'm proud of you for the good grades you're getting and for the other things you do. What if you did it first thing on waking up, before you got moving, so you wouldn't have to break your stride? If you asked me to do something that mattered to you and cost me so little, wouldn't you expect me to do it?"

"I guess so, Mom."

"Why not try it? I think you'll like it."

"I don't know if I'll like it, but okay, I'll try it. I might even start finding things that keep disappearing."

Here, the mother focuses on the specific issue. She doesn't try to tie it in with broader issues of responsibility and self-discipline. She doesn't talk down. She is open in saying that she is asking it for her own sake and not her daughter's. She always acknowledges what's true in her daughter's statements, and asks questions inquiring into her daughter's reasoning and feelings. She sticks to the point, doesn't talk too much, and never interrupts. She also uses an opportunity, in her remark just before the last one, to put her daughter in her position, as a way of getting her daughter to see the situation more clearly.

‖ 4 ‖ Using Questions to Sell Your Ideas

Getting Others to See Your Idea As Different

To some extent, we perform as though we're actors saying the same lines for similiar scenes that we play over and over. The trouble is that often our lines don't quite fit the scene. The present scene is just like an earlier scene in some ways, but different in other important ways. But we look at only the similarities and ignore the differences.

If we looked for the differences, we'd have to change our lines for each scene to make them fit. That takes a lot more thinking and feels more risky. For all change involves risk. So why bother thinking up new lines each time, and take the risk of being wrong in some way, when the old tried ones seem to work well enough? We've gotten into the habit of reacting the same way to situations that seem similar enough to us. We don't examine them carefully enough to see just how similar they are.

When we're selling an idea, we're up against the other person's playing the scene for an old idea that's something like ours but quite different, also. There's always something about a new idea that resembles something in an old one. If an idea were completely new, we couldn't understand it or create it, because we couldn't relate it to anything in our experience. It's only the points of departure that are new.

How can we get the other person to focus on the differences, on the points of departure? How do we get him to think enough, and to take the risk, to create the lines that fit the scene of our idea?

We can do this by asking the right questions. Questions are powerful tools for shaping thinking, making connections, gaining and giving insight, and helping in the release of feelings.

Socrates and Plato, a thinking person's act in ancient Greece, used questions very skillfully, to gain a better understanding of the physical world, society, and the individual.

Asking Questions Requires Some Assertiveness

People often avoid asking questions when selling their ideas, neglecting their most powerful tool. It's hard to ask questions because you know that you're asking for something, rather than giving. And you can ask only so much before you start to irritate the other person. That's why asking a question is an assertive act. People who have little assertiveness find asking difficult.

Let's look more deeply into how to ask questions, because it's the most demanding and also the most rewarding part of selling your ideas. It takes more hard and quick thinking and more self-control than does the planning and organizing, gathering evidence, or balancing benefits against cost. But the gain in doing it is amazing.

Using Questions to Diagnose Objections

In selling your ideas, you need questions largely to reduce the resistance of the other person. When he raises an objection, it's very effective to bring out the line of reasoning that leads him to his objection. You're trying to answer the question, How does he come to his conclusion? Sometimes he won't even know his own line of reasoning until your questions make him think about it.

It's helpful to view any disagreement as a problem for diagnosis. When you've got physical symptoms—pain, dizziness, fatigue, no appetite—you go to the doctor. You're not feeling the way you should. The doctor tries to find out why by asking questions of you and of the lab through tests. Similarly, when an automobile doesn't work as it should, the mechanic asks questions and gets the answers through testing.

When the other person disagrees with you, his objection is a symptom that something's wrong in his thinking or yours. Since your conclusion is different from his, it seems to you that he's not thinking as he should. It's reasonable to assume this since you've done much more thinking and research on your idea than he has. He's probably hearing it for the first time.

Still, it's possible that he knows something that you don't about the objection he raises. So even though his objection doesn't seem to you to be as big a problem as he makes it out to be, you can't be sure until you know his facts and reasoning.

A useful way to start your diagnosis is to view his objection as a symptom that he's not thinking about your idea the way you are. You want to find out where his thinking differs from yours. Is it in a fact, or is it in a part of the reasoning?

To diagnose, you have to use questions: to uncover the other person's reasoning in order to see whether his facts justify his conclusion; and to find out how he knows his facts are true.

Suppose you recommend that the other person use a particular kind of machine because of its benefits. He objects that that kind of machine is no good. First, you might ask him why he thinks it's no good, to see if his facts justify his conclusion. He replies that the machine breaks down a lot.

His answer calls for five more questions from you. These are listed below in their essential form. In parentheses after each question is an example of how to ask the question in a gentle, supportive way rather than a challenging, confronting one. Doing this prevents an interrogation effect.

1. What makes him think that the machine breaks down a lot? ("We have to look into it. Could you tell me what leads you to say that? Because we've never had complaints like that before.")

2. What kinds of breakdowns are they? Because he might be lumping together major breakdowns, which happen infrequently, with occasional minor adjustments that have to be made. ("Would you tell me something about the kinds of breakdowns that have occurred? The reason I ask is that many of these might have just required minor adjustments and weren't real breakdowns.")

3. How often has the machine actually broken down, because maybe what was really a breakdown didn't happen often enough to make the machine no good? ("No one can afford a lot of breakdowns. I'm wondering how often the machine has broken down where it required a repair rather than just an adjustment. Perhaps the real breakdowns happen no more often than is normal.")

4. Did the machine break down because it's defective or because it was used wrong? ("I'm very concerned about finding just where the problem is. Do you suppose I could look into just how the machine was used? Sometimes we don't make it clear enough to the machine operator, and he uses it in a way it's not supposed to be used. That can cause trouble.")

5. How many machines has he had trouble with? Because if it was with only one machine, that one could be a lemon, rather

than that all machines of this kind are no good. ("Could you tell me how many of these machines you've had trouble with? The reason I ask is, if it was only one machine, that could happen with any kind of machine. One defective machine wouldn't really mean that the whole line of that model is bad.")

Suppose, though, in reply to your first question he says that someone he knows who used the machine told him so. Now you move to a question that gets him to reason along with you. You ask him whether the person who told him that the machine is no good told him also the answers to the next four questions. If he didn't, isn't it possible that his conclusion isn't justified?

To ask this gently, you might say: "I'm really concerned about that. I'd like to look into these breakdowns. Did the person who told you this also happen to tell you what kinds of breakdowns they were, how many machines broke down, how often the breakdowns occurred, and how the machines were used? I'm thinking that if you didn't know the answers to these questions when a customer complained about one of your products, isn't it possible that the customer's complaint isn't justified?"

In the following conversation, watch how the one selling the idea continually uses questions to persuade.

"We better leave some lights on while we're away, to discourage burglars."

"We don't need to. We'll only be gone for a few hours."

"That's true, but how long does it take to burglarize a house?"

"Okay, maybe it doesn't take long, but burglars would watch a house before they break in, to see when the people leave."

"Some would, particularly the professionals. But aren't there other burglars who break in on impulse? They see a dark house and they give it a try."

"But burglars know that people leave their lights on when they leave, to fool the burglars."

"Yes, burglars know that some do and some don't. If you were a burglar, wouldn't you feel safer breaking into a dark house than a lighted one, particularly in the early evening?"

"Well, I suppose so. It's just that I hate to spend the money."

"I wouldn't want to spend it either if it were a lot of money. What if it only cost us a quarter?"

"A quarter? Is that all it would be? Which lights should we leave on?"

Giving Insight Through Questions

We generally think of asking questions to *gain* insight. But questions can be used very effectively also to *give* insight by helping the other person to make new connections in his thinking. With your questions you can help him see that things could be related in ways he hadn't noticed before. With your questions, you get him to wonder about and look at things he never thought to consider.

Giving insight is often important in selling ideas. At times, you have to get someone to look at a situation in a new way before he'll buy your idea.

Let's watch a manager using questions to give a supervisor insight into his own behavior so that he can change it.

MANAGER: Tim, it seems to me that your employees would show more initiative, contribute more good ideas, and solve problems better if you didn't supervise them so closely. Whenever I talk to any of your employees about something they're doing, they usually add to their explanations that they checked it out with you first. They tell me this for things they should be deciding for themselves.

SUPERVISOR: I'd like to do that, but they're always coming to me to help them make their decisions. I wish my people were more independent.

MANAGER: Looks like we're aiming at the same thing. Why do you suppose they depend on you to make their decisions for them? Maybe there's something we can do about it.

SUPERVISOR: They're just that way. Some people can work independently; others can't. I seem to have gotten the ones that can't. I'm always having to straighten them out.

MANAGER: Some people do tend to lean on others. Can you give me an example of someone's coming to you with a problem that he should have handled himself? Maybe, without realizing it, you're doing something that encourages them to come to you.

SUPERVISOR: Well, just last week, Bob wasted time looking for me and waiting until I was available just so he could find out if it was okay for him to do the repair on a machine that broke down. He needed it in a hurry and the maintenance department was all tied up. He could have decided that on his own.

MANAGER: What did you tell him when he found you?

SUPERVISOR: Since he asked me, I told him to let maintenance do it.

MANAGER: I don't understand. Why didn't you tell him to use his own judgment? That way you would have encouraged him in this direction.

SUPERVISOR: I already tried that. The last time the same kind of problem came up, I told him to repair it himself but only if he was sure he could do it. I left it for him to decide. As it turned out, he spent two hours on it, couldn't repair it, and then had to give it to maintenance, anyway. I really blew my stack. Blasted the hell out of him. Here I told him to repair it only if he was sure he could do it, but he went ahead with it, anyway.

MANAGER: I guess he wasn't as sure as you wanted him to be. What I'm wondering about is, What else could he have done? How could a person be *sure* he's sure? He could think he's sure and then make a mistake about that. Did you ever think you were sure about something and then turn out to be wrong?

SUPERVISOR: Yeah, it's happened.

MANAGER: So weren't you really bawling him out for not being sure he was sure, which no one could really be? You were telling him he wasn't allowed to make a mistake. Do you think, then, that he would risk making a decision?

SUPERVISOR: I see what you mean. Since I was setting it up so that he couldn't afford to make a mistake, I was actually forcing him to come to me to make his decision for him. I'm going to watch that from now on.

MANAGER: Fine. I think you'll get more initiative and good ideas from your group.

Adjusting Your Questions

Think of the question as an adjustable tool. You can use it with a wide-open setting, so that it calls for a broad range of information; or you can set it to pinpoint the particular fact you want. You need these varied settings in selling ideas, to adjust your questioning to what you're looking for, and to what would be useful in guiding the other person's thinking at the moment.

One way of adjusting a question is for how specific an answer you want. This can range from asking a question that calls for either a yes or a no—such as, Are you married?—to a question that can bring out any kind of information—such as, What's on your mind? And we have such in-between questions as those that ask for a number, a fact, a reason, an intention, a plan, an opinion, or an explanation.

You can also adjust a question for the kind of information you want. In selling your idea, you often want to know the other person's reasoning. When she raises an objection, you want to know what she bases it on. It's important to find this out because she may have a wrong fact or be doing wrong reasoning; on the other hand, maybe she knows something you don't know so that her objection makes sense. This kind of question asks why whether by using the word *why* or its equivalent, such as, What makes you think that? or, How come?

Another kind of information you often need is the quantity or some other specific. You might ask: How much? To what extent? When? Where? Who? or for any other fact that explains her reasoning further.

A third kind of question is the one that introduces new information that the other person didn't include in her thinking. You might start such a question with the words *what if* or *suppose* when you want to know whether an idea you have in mind would take care of her objection. Or you might use such questions as, Did you know? or, Are you aware that? when you're asking if she'll give up her objection in view of this information.

Let's take a look at the use of the question in its various adjustments and forms. Here's a father persuading his teenage son.

"If you would learn to type, you'd save yourself a lot of time now in high school and later in college. And you'd make a better impression with neater papers. Also, you could get higher-paying jobs while at school, and it would help you in your career."

"You're right, Dad, and I'm taking the typing course in school now. Some of the kids thought it'd be boring so they took something else, instead, but I think like you. And since the school offers it, I'm taking it."

"That's good. You're on the right track. How are you coming along in it? You must be most of the way through the course by now." (He starts with a broad question to find out where his son's thinking is. He then knows what to ask about more specifically.)

"Oh, I'm doing all right. I can type without looking at the keys."

"Good. You've got to be able to do that. I'm wondering, are you typing your papers for school? Because I never hear the typewriter going." (Now he asks a specific question based on his son's answer.)

"Not really. I can't type fast enough. It would take me too long. But I'm improving."

"That's good. But are you improving fast enough so that you'll be able to type your papers by the time the course ends? You've only got another month." (He asks a *how much* question.)

"I don't know. I still have to bring up my speed a lot and cut down mistakes. It's harder than you think."

"I'm sure you have to practice a lot. How much practice do you get in class? I'm thinking that maybe you aren't getting enough practice." (Another *how much* question.)

"Well, we have a forty-five-minute class every day and we spend about twenty minutes of that practicing. The teacher explains things the rest of the time."

"That makes an hour and forty minutes a week. With about a month more to go, you should be getting a total of about seven more hours of practice in class. Considering where you are now, do you think seven more hours will enable you to type fast enough and make few enough mistakes so that you'd type your papers? Otherwise, what's the good of the whole course?" (He uses a *how much* question to give insight.)

"I see what you mean. I don't think I'll be able to type that well after only seven more hours of practice. So why am I taking this course if I'm not getting anything out of it? I guess I thought I could do it in this one course."

"I think you're right about needing more than the seven

hours of practice remaining. What if you had thirty-seven more hours of practice? Do you think that you'd type well enough then? What I have in mind is that you practice at home for a half hour a day including weekends for the next two months, in addition to your classes for the next month." (He tries out a new idea with a *what if* question.)

"I don't think I could do that, Dad. I'm so busy now with my courses and being on the school paper and playing in the school orchestra and practicing the violin. I just can't spare the time."

"It's true you'll be pressed some. What if you take a half hour a day out of your movies and TV and phone conversations and visiting for just the next month? Or you could take just fifteen minutes out, and get up fifteen minutes earlier each day. On the weekends you could spare it more easily. After the first month, school would be over and things would be more relaxed." (He uses a *what if* question to look into his son's reasoning.)

"I don't know, Dad. It sounds so hectic. I think I'd get too strained."

"It does sound hectic. What if you were given a good part in a school play and had to spend even more time in learning your part and at rehearsals? Would you feel you'd be too strained to take it?" (Here's a *what if* question to give insight.)

"I have to admit I'd grab it. I see what you mean. It's not a matter of time. It's my motivation."

"Right. Yet don't you think that you'd gain as much from mastering the typing? Once you learned it, you'd always have it because you'd keep it alive by typing whenever you had papers to do. And once you've done enough typing, you'd never lose it, even though you didn't type for a long while. Isn't that worth a half hour a day for just one month while school is on and for one month beyond it when things are more relaxed?" (Here he uses a *how much* question.)

"I guess so.' And I would get a feeling of accomplishment. I'll give it a try." .

"Wonderful. I think you'll be glad you did."

Answering the Questions that Your Questions Raise

When you ask the other person a question, you often create an information gap in her mind. Since people want to see the whole picture around any item of information, they want to know why you're asking. You must have some reasoning in your mind that has a piece missing or you wouldn't be asking a question. They want to know what your reasoning is, just as you want to know the missing piece you're asking about.

To maintain rapport, make your question an exchange of information, not just a request for it. In asking for information you create a desire in the other person to know why you want the information. You should fulfill her desire. Otherwise, she's going to feel that you're asking her to satisfy you without your being willing to satisfy her in return.

Whenever you ask a question, think or say the words *the reason I ask is*, and then continue on with why you're asking. Not only will you be giving to balance your taking, but you'll get better answers. Your question will be much clearer to her once she knows why you want that piece of information. The chances are that she'll give you a richer answer, with information you didn't even think to ask for.

To illustrate how your question can raise questions in the other person's mind, suppose you ask another person, "Why did you do it that way?" You're creating an information gap. He wonders why you're asking. Are you thinking he was foolish to do it that way, or are you admiring what he did and want to know more about it?

In any case, he's uncomfortable because he doesn't know

which it is. He's likely then to jump to a conclusion about it, depending on what he expects from you, and on his confidence in his own judgment. Either way you lose some rapport, because you've made him uneasy, and in addition, you might irritate him if he thinks you're criticizing him.

If you keep in mind the phrase *the reason I ask is* whenever you ask a question, and if the way he did it looks good to you and you want to know more about it, you could add to your question, "It might be a better way than the one we usually use. I'd like to look into it."

On the other hand, if you disapprove, you could add: "You didn't use the regular procedure, which you were asked to follow. I'm wondering if you had some special reason for not doing it our usual way."

When you ask questions without telling why you're asking, you impose an interrogation effect. This makes the other person both anxious that he might say the wrong thing, and angry that you're treating him like an object to squeeze information from.

You can almost feel the irritation that the questions arouse in the following discussion:

"We ought to set up a small library in our department. That way the people would read more, get new ideas, and keep abreast of what's going on generally in our kind of activity, because the literature is so available. They might not bother to go to the company library for this."

"It would cost too much. We don't have the money for this kind of thing."

"How much could we spend for this?"

"Very little. Less than it would cost. The budget is tight."

"How much do you think it will cost?"

"I don't know. I haven't even thought about it."

"Well, what makes you think it will cost too much?"

"Books are expensive and so are magazine subscriptions. Besides, the people won't read them. I don't want them taking time off the job, and they're not going to read them in the evening or on weekends when they could be watching TV, or doing anything else they like, or even chores."

"How do you know that a lot of them wouldn't enjoy reading more about their jobs?"

"Oh, c'mon. If they're going to read, they'd rather read a mystery or a magazine, or watch TV or a movie, or go out somewhere. Anyway, we don't have the room for a library."

"How much room would we need?"

"How should I know? You're the one who suggested it, you tell me."

"How do you know, then, that we couldn't fit it in?"

"Hell, we're so crowded here as it is. Listen, I feel kind of badgered, or is it just hot in here. Anyway, I've got a meeting I have to prepare for, so we'll have to table this."

Listen to how much easier discussing it is when you tell why you're asking. Let's start just after the opening remark:

"It would cost too much. We don't have the money for this kind of thing."

"Building a whole library would cost too much. How much do you think we could afford? I was thinking of starting real small and gradually building it."

"I don't know. I'd have to look at our budget. It would still cost money, which I'd have to take from something else."

"It would cost a little, but suppose we started with maybe half a dozen books and three magazine subscriptions, and maybe put up a few shelves to store them. Could we manage that?"

"Maybe, but even if we could, nobody's going to read the books and magazines. We don't want them reading while they're working, and they're not going to read them at home when they could be watching TV or reading something more exciting, or doing the chores they have to do."

"There is a lot of competition for their time, and some people wouldn't read any of the material. But do you think that perhaps some others would read a little of the literature, while still others might read a lot? Different people are interested in different topics and a number of them might do a little reading during part of their lunch or coffee breaks, or while they're traveling. And they might recommend particular articles and book chapters to each other."

"Well, even if they did, where are we going to store this material? We're crowded as it is. We don't have any space for a library."

"Yes, we are tight on space. Why couldn't we put up some shelves in the conference room, and add them as we need them? I measured the space, and we can easily accommodate five shelves, eight feet wide, on each of two walls. This would last us quite a while. Before we used up anywhere near this space, we'd be throwing out old issues of the magazines."

"All right, I'll consider it."

A good rule to follow in asking questions is to not ask a question unless you know why you're asking and can tell it to the other person. If you can't put your finger on why you're asking, the chances are the question is not worth asking. You haven't worked out where you're going with your questioning. Generally, you won't gain enough to justify your making the demand for information, and maybe irritating the other person.

Our Emotions Stop Us from Asking About Others' Objections

We have to draw a bit on our self-confidence in order to ask questions that serve our own purpose. For asking such a question makes a demand that can vary in strength from requesting simple ordinary facts, through probing and exposing, to challenging and confronting.

Even the everyday question asking what time it is requires the other person to interrupt his thoughts or conversation, read his watch, decide whether to tell the time to the nearest minute or five minutes, and give you his finding. Asking him to give his opinion on how something's going to turn out, whether it be an election, a job, a ball game, or a love affair, requests him to think, to make a decision, to commit himself, and to risk being wrong.

Asking someone for her reaction to a particular person, a speech, a business deal, or a movie is to ask her to reveal herself a little. For her reactions tell something about her attitudes, values, interests, and beliefs. And asking her for her reasoning can be challenging, for it tests her competence. Are her facts true? Is her logic sound?

Inquiring into another person's objection requires guts, for the question might very well be confronting him with the realization that he's wrong, and that this might be revealed.

When you ask the other person why he thinks his objection is justified in view of your contradictory evidence, he knows that he has to produce better evidence than you have or else back away from his objection. He might have objected casually, or on a gut basis, and doesn't have much evidence. Yet backing away could make him seem impulsive or dishonest in raising his objection, and might cause him to lose face.

People can have all kinds of emotional reactions to asking another person a question. They can feel anxious that they'll make the other person angry if the question embarrasses him; or they might feel guilty about possibly inconveniencing the other person; or they might be angry that they have to ask the question.

When people ask a question that requires the other person to justify what he said, they often feel that it makes the other person view them as an adversary. The question sets up a moment of conflict between them. Suddenly, it's as though they're in a chess game and the question is a threatening piece.

This question that asks the other person for the reasoning

behind his objection is one of the most difficult, emotionally, to ask. Often, people avoid asking it and defeat themselves, for they've abandoned one of the most powerful, versatile tools for selling ideas.

To sell your idea effectively, you need to keep in touch with your feelings so that you can know what they are at the moment and prevent their pushing you away from asking questions.

Think of the question not as a weapon, but as a tool helping people to think straight and to make the best decision. Think of yourself not as the other person's opponent, but as his partner in deciding about the idea.

Try to stay relaxed during the discussion. Learn some relaxation techniques and apply them when selling your ideas, particularly when you face an objection and want to ask a question about it.

The technique of telling why you're asking the question is very helpful in softening the question, making it easy for the other person to deal with it.

‖ 5 ‖ Taking Objections Apart

The Strong Urge to
Tie Things Together

In learning how to live, from infancy on, we're continually trying to figure out which goes with what for the many things happening around us. We want to know what things are related to each other. For this means we understand, and understanding gives us power.

What exactly are we trying to understand? We want to know what causes a particular thing to happen. Knowing what causes something enables us to predict when it will happen. For whenever we spot the cause of a particular happening, we know the happening will follow. Often, knowing the cause enables us to *control* the happening. For if we can bring about the cause, we can make the happening occur.

Our minds are attuned from birth onward to make connections among the things we encounter. We're constantly striving to see relationships so we can understand what causes what, predict what's going to happen, and control what's controllable. But we can't do this just by seeing relationships among particular things. To get the power that comes from understanding, we need to know the relationships among *kinds* of things. Generalizations describe these relationships.

Our knowledge that lower temperature causes food to last longer enables us to store perishable food. Knowing that insults cause anger, we're able to avoid antagonizing people by controlling our impulses.

That's why we love generalizations so much. We form them when there's the slightest hint of a relationship. They make us feel in the know. Two things happen together, and immediately, like gossips who observe a flirtation, we see a relationship. Sometimes, however, we see one of these things happening without the other, and we don't know anymore whether our generalization is true.

In forming these generalizations, we're often filling information gaps by imagining what belongs there, from the information we have from past experiences and from wishes. We're jumping to conclusions. After all, we don't know if the two things always go together or if what we observed is an accidental occurrence.

The first time we hear a siren, we see that it comes from a police car. We then form the following generalization: If a siren sounds, there must be a police car going by. We're filling the information gaps about how the police car and the siren are related, just with assumptions. We don't know at that point whether all police cars have sirens or just that one; but because we love generalizations we assume it's all police cars. We also don't know if sirens are on only police cars or on other vehicles as well. We assume just police cars because if we allow for other vehicles, it leaves us with the uncomfortable gap, What other vehicles? which is more difficult to fill.

The next time we hear a siren, we see that it comes from a fire truck. Then we change our generalization by adding fire truck to police car. Then one day we see the siren sound coming from an ambulance and we add that, or we change our generalization to make the source of the siren sound any vehicle that has to get somewhere in a hurry and has the authority to signal others to get out of the way.

If the first flower we encounter smells sweet, we expect the same from all other flowers. Again, we fill the gap of whether all flowers have a sweet smell. If in our encounters with flowers all of them smell sweet, we would have to encounter a number of exceptions rather than just one before we gave up our generalization.

We form the generalization about two things going together from our encountering them together, such as: a teacher and being criticized in an embarrassing way for performing poorly ("teachers don't understand children"); achieving athletically and being praised by teammates ("playing sports gives people self-confidence"): making a costly error because someone gives us wrong information ("you can't trust anyone's information"). Again, we filled in gaps about whether it happens in all cases and under what conditions in order to form generalizations.

Each of us experiences a different very small fraction of what goes on in the world. From that different very small fraction, each of us fills gaps to make our personal generalizations about the world. That's why we all wind up with different generalizations. This means we each see the world differently, make different predictions about what's going to happen in the same situation, and try to control situations in different ways. Some ways work out well; others fail.

Filling Information Gaps Unrealistically

We continually experience the following kinds of information gaps about different kinds of information: what happened? including all the specifics; what caused it? what will result? and what motivated someone? When we experience information gaps, we often fill them in a way that makes us feel good, or fits the way we feel about the world. We do this rather than face realistically that we don't know what belongs in the gap, and that we're just making an assumption.

A woman insists to her child over his protest that he put on a sweater when he goes out to play so that he won't catch a cold. She assumes that being cold causes a cold rather than facing her information gap and finding out that colds are caused by viruses coming from a person who has a cold and is in close contact.

A man who's missing his comb from his bureau, where he normally puts it each night when he empties his pockets, mutters angrily, "Who took my comb?" He doesn't consider that he might have mislaid it himself.

A manager resists a proposed idea right off with the objection "We tried that before and it didn't work." She jumps to the conclusion that the proposed idea is just like the past idea, rather than asking about differences. There might be a critical difference that could make the idea work.

An employee rejects his supervisor's criticism without examining it. The employee feels that his supervisor dislikes him and that this is the reason for the criticism. A job applicant whom I interviewed for a client company advised me not to contact a particular former superior because the superior disliked him, had it in for him, and would give him a bad rating. The former superior told me that he was amazed by the applicant's remark because, the former superior said, he had praised the applicant and requested a raise for him.

There are plenty of information gaps—enough to enable each person to view the world in his own unique way. He can fill the gaps with his assumptions and feel reasonable whenever no one has the facts to contradict him, only other assumptions of their own to suit their purposes. This enables each person to see the world as he wants to, by inventing facts, causes, predictions, and motivations to fit the preconceptions he's comfortable with, and to support his self-esteem.

Using Reasoning to
Prevent Bad Decisions

Since people have the strong urge to fill information gaps with assumptions, and since these assumptions are often based on wishes rather than on the way things really are, errors in judgment and wrong decisions are frequently made. Fortunately, everyone has a powerful tool for preventing filling gaps in this way. The tool is reasoning ability. But, unfortunately, it's much neglected.

The laws of logic reflect how the world works. We've all acquired knowledge of these laws just from living and observing what happens. So we can reason quite well. But too often we avoid logic, particularly when it carries us to conclusions we don't like.

When people want something badly enough, they invent the assumptions and make the reasoning errors they need to support their case. Generally, there's still enough room left for a little correct reasoning. The correct reasoning part gives them the illusion that they're being reasonable.

They need this illusion. They know that people rely on reasoning to make decisions because the laws of logic reflect the world as it really is. Operating by these laws leads to gains, and violating them, to losses. People apply the test of reason so that they won't make decisions impulsively, and lose out. Using reason rather than impulse also gives them the reassuring feeling that they're in control of themselves.

Listen to this fragment of conversation.

"We ought to trade in our car for a new one. I know it's only two years old, but this fellow I met trades every two years.

He told me how much he comes out ahead that way, and I was impressed."

"How many miles does he drive a year?"

"I don't know, but it's probably about the same amount as I drive since we both live about the same distances from our jobs."

The person who proposed the idea is making an unwarranted assumption: Their driving mileages for other purposes are also the same. When he starts with this error, he makes himself feel good in two ways: He can reason correctly the rest of the way; and he comes out with the conclusion he wants. However, his conclusion that he should trade in his car every two years is wrong because he started wrongly, but he ignores this.

This ability to ignore error is another way that the human is superior to the machine. The human is more flexible. The machine follows its instructions and always gets the right answer except when it breaks down. The human is much more versatile. He can work into his thinking the errors he needs while denying to himself that he's doing it, and come out with whatever answer serves his purpose.

Someday, someone will build a machine with this capability. When that happens, watch out. For man will have created an enemy worse than himself.

Listen to this bit of wrong reasoning.

"Alice is leaving the job."

"What happened? She's really a great worker."

"She says that she's not developing new skills in this job. She doesn't have a chance to grow and get ahead."

"Give her more money."

"But she didn't mention money."

"It doesn't matter whether she mentions it or not. It's what they all want, and what keeps them on a job."

The person who suggested giving more money made an

unsupported assertion, which is another common reasoning error. Starting with the assumption that money is the overriding motivator for all people, he then reasons correctly that giving her more will cause her to stay. However, his conclusion that she'll stay is wrong if his premise is wrong, that everyone is really motivated by money no matter what they say.

Now let's listen to a further conversation between these same two people after the situation with Alice is resolved.

"What happened with Alice?"

"I offered her more money and she decided to stay. She also asked me to try to find some way to broaden her job so she would develop new skills and could grow. I told her I would think about it. Boy, am I relieved."

"See, I told you people are motivated in the job by the money they make. Here's proof. You offered her more and she stayed."

"But how do you know she was motivated by this? Maybe she reconsidered and decided that first she'd stay and try hard to get the kind of job she wants at our place, since she likes other things here, like the people she works with, and this industry."

"Because money is the name of the game. That's what gets people to work in a job."

Here the person who suggests giving Alice more money makes two reasoning errors. The first error is circular reasoning. He reasons that Alice's staying on the job proves that his generalization is true, that money alone motivates people to work at a particular job. Then he circles back by reasoning that his generalization explains why Alice stayed on the job. His second reasoning error is generalizing from a single instance. He does this when he gives the single instance of Alice's staying as the proof of his generalization.

Another reasoning error we have to watch for is attacking

the source of the idea rather than the idea itself. Here's an example:

"Joe says we ought to increase the insurance on our house. With the way house prices have increased the last few years he feels that our insurance wouldn't cover replacing it if it ever burned down."

"Listen, Joe sells home insurance. What else would you expect him to say?"

Here, the person responding, instead of discussing the idea, attacks the person who presented it, on the basis of his having a self-serving motivation. Now, listen to this variation.

"Joe is overly anxious about everything right now. His marriage is breaking up and he's very worried. I don't know how reliable his judgment is."

Again, the person responding argues against the idea by attacking the person who presented it as being incompetent for the time being, rather than talking about the idea itself. Neither the facts nor the reasoning of the idea are discussed.

A very common reasoning error is all-or-none thinking. A person making this error says that either all people or things or situations are a certain way or that none are, rather than considering that some are and some aren't. Here's an illustration:

"I don't see any point in giving our managers a course in how to counsel their subordinates. Either a manager is good at talking with and helping subordinates, or he isn't, so a course won't do any good."

"You can't make expert counselors of all managers, but don't you think that some managers can become a little better than they are now?"

"I guess some of them can, but you can't change people anyway so what good does it do?"

"Well, it's true that you can't change everyone in every way, but haven't you ever seen someone change a little for the better in some ways?"

"Well, yes, I've seen some changes, but not a lot. Anyway, the courses offered are no good."

"It's true that some courses aren't, but aren't there likely to be some that are? Some of our departments have sent people a number of times to one of these courses in counseling and they've spoken highly of it."

"I guess so. We'll send someone and evaluate it on our own."

A reasoning error that occurs frequently is to assume that one thing causes another because they happen together. Take a look at this conversation.

DON: I read recently that people who exercise more eat less. They actually found this to be true. I would have expected the opposite.

CAROL: I can understand that. When a person exercises, he discharges tension. And tension causes people to eat more. So with less tension, he eats less.

JIM: That's not how it happens. In order to get yourself to exercise and also to eat less, you need more self-discipline. When a person is under stress, he has less control of himself. But at other times in his life he has more control so he's able to both exercise and also eat less. It isn't the exercise that causes less eating. It's the greater self-control that causes both the ability to exercise and the reduction in eating. Would you pass me another doughnut, please, the jelly-filled one this time.

CAROL: You must be under a lot of stress. I guess it's the tension you build up from not exercising. Don't you think the French cruller will relax you more?

DON: You've both got this wrong. It's the lowered eating that causes the exercise rather than the other way around. Eating less causes tension. The increased tension causes people to exercise more in order to let out the tension. I'll try the chocolate-covered one since I don't want to strain myself with exercise. It makes me anxious.

CAROL: Which causes which is a tricky problem. But one thing I'm sure of from what I've observed here is that arguing causes eating.

JIM: You're pouncing on the obvious. You've got to look further. Actually, it's tension that causes both arguing and eating. I think we'd better send for some more food. Otherwise, we'll never get this worked out. We'll be too tense.

Another problem in reasoning together is defining words differently. Two people can be arguing over whether doing a particular thing is too costly where one person is evaluating cost on the basis of what you get back and the other is measuring the cost by what's available to spend.

Analyzing an Objection

To deal with an objection effectively, you first have to understand it fully. An objection consists of three parts: the facts; the reasoning from the facts; and the conclusion arrived at from the reasoning. To understand the objection, you have to know all three.

Generally, the other person tells you only part of her objection. She'll almost always tell you her conclusion, which is how she presents her objection. She may add part or all of the facts and reasoning. You've got to get from her what's missing.

Whenever part of her objection is missing, you'll be tempted to fill it in based on what you imagine she means. You've got to resist that. When you find yourself thinking, she probably means such and such, you're risking misunderstanding.

A fact is something that's directly observed. A conclusion is reasoned to from facts and/or earlier conclusions. The price of a piece of equipment is a fact. You see it on the price tag or in the catalog, or hear it from the seller. Your decision that it's too expensive is a conclusion based perhaps on your reasoning from the fact of how much it costs and your conclusion that something bad will happen if you spend that much. There is a greater chance of an error in a conclusion than there is in a fact, since a conclusion could have something wrong with the reasoning behind it as well as with the facts.

The following statements illustrate the difference between a fact and a conclusion:

1. John got home at eight o'clock. He must have, because he left here at 7:30 and it's a half hour from here to his home. (Conclusion, because it was reasoned to from the facts.)

2. John got home at eight o'clock. I know because I saw him come in and the eight o'clock news was just coming on. (Fact, because it was directly observed.)

3. My employees won't like that because making changes upsets them. (Conclusion. She might have reasoned to this based on the fact that she observed that they were upset when the last two changes were made. While the fact might be correct, her reasoning could be wrong in that her employees might have been upset because the particular changes were bad, not because changes were made.)

4. The capacity of that machine is lower than that of our other machines. (Fact, if based on either the manufacturer's rating or on a direct observation.)

5. From the look of that equipment, it won't last long. (Conclusion, because what's observed is the appearance, perhaps

worn parts. That it won't last long is reasoned to from its appearance.)

To evaluate the other person's objection, you have to inquire into the facts and reasoning until you bring out the whole picture of that objection. This means asking questions. If the logic of the objection doesn't hold up, the other person is likely to become more interested in your idea, or else will retreat to another objection. You then have to inquire into this next objection. Let's look at Dan's inquiries into Mary's objections.

DAN: I think we ought to put Jack in charge of that new project as supervisor. He certainly has the technical knowledge, and he gets along well with others.

MARY: I don't know, Dan. It's hard for me to picture Jack as a leader. He is bright and conscientious, and he has good technical knowledge for the job. But he isn't aggressive. He doesn't express himself forcefully enough. He's too quiet. [Conclusion: To be a leader, you must express yourself forcefully rather than quietly.]

DAN: He doesn't come on strong, but why do you think a person has to express himself forcefully to be a good leader? I noticed that many of the people come to him for advice. [Asks for the basis of Mary's conclusion that a leader must be forceful.]

MARY: That's just it. I think they come to him because they just want someone to listen to them, and Jack's the kind of guy who can't say no, can't turn them away. They just use up his time. [Conclusion.]

DAN: He does have a gentle way about him but how do you know that he wants to turn them away any more than he does? Isn't it just as likely that he feels he should be helping them? Jane told me that when she worked with Jack on a project, Jack stuck to his guns if Jane didn't have a better argument. But Jack always listened to Jane's ideas. Jane really enjoyed working with Jack. [Asks for Mary's reasoning supporting her conclusion that Jack can't turn the people away.]

MARY: Oh, I'm sure he feels he should be helping them, but that's not enough. A good supervisor has to know how much help to give and when to stop helping. He has to be able to say no. And he has to be able to insist that something be done when an employee doesn't want to do it. [Conclusions that would be accepted.] I'm not sure he's able to do those things. He just isn't forceful enough. [Conclusions that are questionable.]

DAN: If by forceful you mean speaking in a commanding tone, it's true, Jack's not forceful. Have you ever known any really good supervisors who were also quiet and gentle in their manner? [Dan's question asks if Mary has encountered any facts—really good supervisors who were quiet and gentle—that contradict her conclusion that forcefulness is essential.]

MARY: I guess I've known a few, but they've been pretty rare compared to the many forceful ones I've known. [Fact based on her observation.]

DAN: The forceful ones seem to be more common. But if something's rare, does that mean it's bad?

MARY: Listen, you've made some good points. It's possible that Jack would make a good supervisor. It's just that I can't recall hearing Jack insist on or oppose anything in an aggressive way. [Fact.]

DAN: A supervisor has to be aggressive enough. But isn't it

possible that Jack is sufficiently persuasive in a patient, reasonable way so that he doesn't have to get into loud conflicts? This is the impression I get from talking to people who worked with him. [Questions Mary's unsupported assertion that you have to be loudly aggressive to be a good leader.]

MARY: Dan, you make a convincing case. All right, let me take a closer look to see if, with all his quietness, he's really a strong leader.

Why It's Important to Have
Evidence Against the Objection

In inquiring into an objection, you're trying to find out how the other person knows his objection is so. What makes him think that? How did he arrive at it?

Often, he objects on a gut basis with little evidence to support his objection. On top of that, he may not even realize how little evidence he has. If you just ask him what makes him think his objection is so, he may develop a vague answer that sounds perfectly adequate to him.

But when you add evidence that contradicts his objection, to explain why you're asking, he may first realize how weak his support is for his objection. You've planned and done research on your idea; he's just hearing about it now.

Suppose you suggest to someone that he start a particular project because it could save his department seven thousand dollars a year. He replies, "It sounds like a good idea but I think we should put it off for now, considering all the other things we're working on." If you were to just ask, "Why don't we put it ahead of another project?" he could very easily reply, "Because the other projects are all too important." But suppose you add to your question the following evidence for putting the project ahead of another one: "We'd finish it in six weeks at a one-time cost of seven thousand dollars. This gives us a return of one hundred percent. Wouldn't it be worthwhile to put it ahead of a project that brings a much lower return?" He can't just reply that the other projects are too important.

Look at the following case:

PAUL: We'd make fewer hiring errors if two other people in the department, in addition to the supervisor, were to interview each job applicant above the clerical level. The two other people would provide their input, but the supervisor would make the decision. That way we'd get the benefit of three evaluations of each applicant rather than just one.

JANET: We can't afford the time. At an average of an hour per interview, we'd be spending three times as many employee-hours on each applicant. That's too much. After all, our department hires about twenty people a year.

PAUL: That is a fair amount of time. What would you say is the average number of job applicants we interview for each job?

JANET: Probably about four, after personnel does their screening. That would still use up too much time.

PAUL: It would mean an extra eight hours per applicant. How many of those twenty people a year we've been hiring turn out to be hiring mistakes? I'm asking because it might still be worth it, considering how much it costs to make a mistake.

JANET: About a quarter of them are hiring mistakes. Either we let them go or they leave on their own because they're not suited to the job. But we should never have hired them in the first place.

PAUL: That makes about five hiring mistakes a year. When you consider how costly it is to make a hiring mistake, wouldn't it be worth it to do an extra eight employee-hours of interviewing for each person hired, to prevent such a mistake? The extra eight employee-hours comes from two additional people's interviewing four applicants for each job opening.

Our hero makes an all-or-none reasoning error by assuming that three interviewers instead of one would enable them to avoid *all* the hiring mistakes. Actually, the multiple interviews are likely to avoid only a portion of the mistakes. Unfortunately, Paul's reasoning error could cause him to lose more credibility than he deserves. For Janet, in turn, might very well make the reasoning error of generalizing that Paul's reasoning must be faulty generally, based on this single instance. For Janet, everything Paul offers in support of his idea becomes suspect. Our hero has stumbled for the moment but he perseveres.

JANET: Having three interviewers isn't going to make the difference in all cases. For some of the applicants, the same mistake would still be made. But I'm not sure that three would be better than one, anyway. I've seen lots of cases where two employees side with each other against the third when they're trying to carry out a task. It's the same with juries where maybe three hold out for a while against the other nine, and then one by one they come around to the majority view. If the other two disagree with the supervisor, he might feel pressured to come around to their point of view.

Here, Janet makes the reasoning error of using a false analogy. She is arguing that because all three situations are alike in that they have a number of people participating in the making of a decision, they're alike in all ways. Paul focuses on this error in his inquiry.

PAUL: The other two might influence the supervisor's decision. But isn't this situation different from the other two you mentioned? Here, the supervisor is the only one responsible for the decision and he's the only one who gains or loses by it. In the other two situations, there is a shared responsibility. So isn't the supervisor likely to take into account their viewpoints, and take a close second look at his own if there's disagreement, which is what we want? But he won't be pressured because he's responsible.

JANET: That's a good point, but there's another problem. If the other two people are poorer interviewers than the supervisor is, the average effectiveness of the three will be lower than that of the supervisor alone. So how are we going to make sure the other two are as good or better than the supervisor?

Janet makes another reasoning error that we didn't discuss before: reasoning from a principle that doesn't apply. The principle she's using is: The average of three different figures is lower than the highest of the three figures. The principle is obviously true, but it doesn't apply here, as Paul points out in his next remark. This error makes her conclusion wrong. She then compounds her error by asking a question based on the assumption that her false conclusion is true. But watch our hero nimbly unravel the tangle, with his inquiry into Janet's reasoning error.

PAUL: Yes, if we were averaging the interviewing skills, we could easily wind up with a lower one. But how do you figure we'd be averaging them? The supervisor would be making the decision. He'd just be getting additional information. So we'd actually be adding skills rather than averaging them. And wouldn't any addition make the sum of the three skills greater than that of the supervisor alone? We wouldn't have to worry about whether the other two are as good as the supervisor.

A person's reasoning from a principle that doesn't apply is tricky to deal with. The other person tends to look for something wrong in the principle rather than for whether it applies. Generally, he has to agree that the principle is right, so he gives way to a false argument. But Paul was alert and asked the right question.

JANET: Maybe you're right, Paul. I have been bothered by so many hiring mistakes. Applying teamwork to hiring could give us an edge.

‖ 6 ‖ Breaking Through the Personal Premises Barrier

Hotels generally post rules like the following ones. In parentheses after each rule is what's implied might happen if you violate the rule.

Do not swim in the pool without a lifeguard present (because you might drown if you do).

Checkout time is 12:00 noon. (You will be charged extra if you check out later without permission to do so.)

Please play your TV's softly after 10:00 P.M. (or else people in neighboring rooms will complain about you and we'll have to complain to you).

These rules are premises enabling you to reason to what's likely to happen if you violate them. They each tell a cause and its effect. Each of us carries within him thousands of personal rules that are premises we reason from. They tell us what to expect from any occurrence.

We developed these personal premises from the way we

interpreted experiences from birth onward. We tend to generalize each of our experiences, to form a premise from which we reason further. Later experiences that give results similar to earlier ones strengthen the influence of the premises we've formed. When we have another experience where there isn't enough information to determine whether it supports or contradicts a premise we've already formed based on our experience, we tend to interpret the experience as supporting that premise.

Suppose we have some experiences similar to the following: Someone asks us to do him a favor. We oblige. Some time after that we ask him for a favor and he turns us down without any justification. We might then generalize to form the premise: *It doesn't pay to do someone a favor since he won't return the favor.*

Now suppose we have the same experience with another person, but this time it's not clear to us whether circumstances make it impossible for him to return the favor, or he chooses to turn us down. We're likely to interpret his turndown as deliberate since this supports our premise. Another person, having more favorable experiences, would form the opposite premise as follows: *If you do a favor for someone, he'll return the favor.*

Let's consider some other personal premises and how they affect your selling your ideas. Someone may have the premise: *If I make a decision without talking it over with someone, it's likely to be wrong.* In selling your idea to this person, you're not likely to get a decision in one meeting with him unless there's someone else present he can talk to about it. Otherwise, he'll have to find someone to discuss it with before he gives you an answer.

You in turn may hold the premise: *If the other person doesn't decide right off about the idea I'm trying to sell him, he's likely to reject my idea.* This could cause you to put pressure on the other person to come to a quicker decision than is realistic. He may then become irritated, feeling that you're impatient to have your way and that you're not concerned about making the right decision.

He doesn't know about the premise that's driving you, and that you're worried that your idea will be rejected.

A person may hold the premise *If the other person asks me what I base my conclusion on, it means that my thinking is not trustworthy.* Since this person is sensitive about whether others trust his thinking, he may continually test others on this. He might withhold the basis of his conclusion when he gives it, and resist answering when he's asked to give his reasoning. He wants to see if the other person will let him by, as a sign of trust. It's helpful when asking questions to tell him that you want to increase your understanding, get a clearer picture, as a way of reassuring him that you're not checking his thinking.

We're generally not aware of our personal premises. If we try hard to figure out our reason for deciding a certain way, we might become conscious of some of them. We tend to hide them from ourselves, particularly when they offend our self-image, and conceal them even more so from others.

Let's look at how personal premises can affect the decision on a specific idea. Here is a father trying to sell an idea to his son who has just started working in his first career job. Personal premises that could be the basis of a remark are in brackets following it:

FATHER: You could save a lot of money by shining your own shoes. You keep them well-shined, so you must be taking a lot of shines. With shines costing so much, it really pays to do it yourself. [Buying services that you could perform yourself is wasteful.]

SON: Listen, Dad. I just couldn't do as good a job as they do. They're pros. They do it all the time. They know the tricks and they've got the right stuff. All I'd get are dull-looking shoes and I'd be wasting a lot of time. [People who make a living at something can do it much better than others.]

FATHER: So you'll read the directions and you'll do it, too. What do you think it takes, a college degree in shoe shining? Stop kidding yourself. You're just being lazy. You don't want to put yourself out. [Two personal premises might be influencing this response: a) If a person doesn't want to do something that requires some effort, it's because he's lazy; and b) when a person doesn't admit why he's doing something he shouldn't be doing, tell him what's really motivating him to straighten him out.]

SON: Who the hell are you calling lazy? I get good grades and have a job after school and do my chores around the house. Now let me explain something to you. My shoes are always shined and I dress neatly, too. It shows others that I think enough of myself to figure that I deserve being well-dressed. It also shows I care enough about others to want them to think well of me. That's how you get ahead. [Two personal premises suggested by this remark are: a) Dressing well impresses others; and b) impressing others is the way to get ahead.]

FATHER: Calm down, calm down, I'm only trying to help you. You can have shined shoes all the time and still save a lot of money. You just buy a bottle of liquid polish and dab it on with an applicator. Takes a minute. And you get a real good shine. I use it myself.

SON: Listen, Dad, I know you're trying to help me but it's just not my style. Just dabbing some polish on isn't going to give me the kind of shine I want. I'll get polish on my hands and it won't wash off, and my hands will look dirty. You and I just do some things differently. What's right for you isn't right for me and vice versa. [Anything I do with my hands isn't likely to work out right.]

Personal Premises Work Against
Thinking in Specifics

Personal premises are generalizations that describe a relationship between two things and are particular to the individual. If you do that, this happens. "This happens" can refer to a tangible result or to the fact that you're doing something good or bad. Doing something good or bad can be part of another premise that says doing something good or bad results in your feeling good or bad, or that you'll be praised or punished, or that you'll gain or lose.

The individual's personal premises guide him in predicting. They are formed out of his experiences and personality. They tell what he expects to happen in all kinds of circumstances: if a particular political party gets elected, if he tells a lie, if he lends money, if he takes certain kinds of risks, if he treats people in certain ways. In just about every kind of situation, his personal premises tell him what to expect and therefore point the way in his deciding.

The optimist and the pessimist have opposite personal premises for many kinds of situations. The optimist harbors such personal premises as: I impress people favorably; when I take a chance, it works out well; the future is promising. He then reasons from these personal premises to what's likely to happen when he meets a new person, takes a risk, or contemplates what the outcome will be. The pessimist, holding opposite personal premises, reasons to opposite conclusions.

Since personal premises are generalizations, they often close our minds to the specifics. Yet the specifics often make all the difference. Generalizations tell us in what way a number of different things are alike. We use our personal premise to reason from, so that we know what to expect whenever we encounter something that's covered by this generalization. But we have to make a concentrated effort to get at the specifics of these things in order to find out how they're different, and what effects these differences have.

Look at the following conversation:

"I've got some money I'd like to invest, and what I need is some good advice on how to invest it. My premise on this is, if you want advice on where to invest your money, ask a rich person. So I'm going to see Lynn tomorrow."

"Your premise might be good generally, but did you know that Lynn inherited her money and has been losing it in the stock market?"

"What! I didn't know that. I'm glad you told me. I'll see Steve, instead. He made it big on his own."

"That's true. But Steve made it big by being an engineering genius and creating some hi-tech products and selling them. He's making a lot of money but he's losing a good bit of it back. His favorite way of losing is in real estate ventures."

"I'm glad I talked to you. I'll see Diane. She's really living big. She must know how to grow money."

"Diane married into money. She might give you some tips on how to get a rich husband, that is, if your husband doesn't mind."

"Looks like my premise is shot. What premise guides you on this?"

"Mine is, look at the specifics of each case. Don't just follow a general premise."

How Networks of Personal Premises Influence Our Behavior

We take for granted the rightness of the personal premises that we hold deeply. We seldom question them. These are the ones we've lived with and followed for so long that they seem natural to us. That's the way things are. To violate them seems to us to be unrealistic and risky.

Other personal premises are superficial and are easily changed. After holding the premise that Brand X is better than other brands, one day we change from Brand X to Brand Y just because of someone's urging us to try it or because the store is out of Brand X. This kind of premise has little power to motivate us.

Personal premises that have high power are those that are linked with other premises. Then, changing one premise affects a whole network of premises. Since personal premises guide a person's reactions, abandoning a whole network of them leaves a person anxious and uncertain about what to do in a great variety of situations.

Here's a conversation that isn't likely to happen. But to illustrate a network of personal premises, let's suppose the person revealing his feelings has a great deal of insight into himself and is quite willing to reveal it.

"I'm sorry to be so late with my reports. The problem is that Ann is continually late in getting me the information I need."

"I see. Have you talked to her about her lateness and the trouble it's causing?"

"Oh, no. I couldn't do that. It's too risky to criticize someone. [Personal premise.] It's always better to praise. [Personal premise.] In fact, I praised her for the information she provided even though it wasn't all that good."

"Why did you do that? And what's so risky about criticizing when someone deserves it?"

"Well, people won't like me if I criticize them, and will if I praise them." [Personal premise.]

"Why are you so concerned about her liking you?"

"If people don't like you, they won't help you. You can't depend on them." [Personal premise.]

"Why do you have to depend on them so much? What kind of help do you need?"

"Any kind I can get. I'm a weak and dependent person." [Personal premise.]

These premises are all tied together. One results from another. It would be difficult to persuade this person to criticize someone since he would have to change all these premises. It's hard to reach such a deeply held premise as that he is weak and dependent.

Such a premise may also give rise to another chain of premises that lead him to prefer a strong, dominating leader over a democratic one since the dominating one would tell him very specifically what to do. The democratic leader would often ask him to use his own judgment, which he has little confidence in.

Let's see how you might deal with this situation realistically, based on what the other person is more likely to say.

"I'm sorry to be so late with my reports. The problem is that Ann is continually late in getting me the information I need."

"I see. Have you talked to her about this?"

"Yes, I have. She said she has so many other things to do that she can't help it at times. The trouble is, it happens all the time."

"What did you say to her then?"

"Well, I told her how important it is to get these reports in on time, and that I couldn't do it without her information. She said the other things she was doing were important, too, but that she would try to do better. So we'll have to see now if she does."

"Did you ask her what things she's doing are more important than these reports? Maybe she has a misunderstanding both about the use of these reports and about the importance of some of her other things."

"No, I didn't. Perhaps I should have. But I didn't want to imply that she doesn't know what she's doing." [Personal premise: Asking another person to justify what he's doing amounts to destructive criticism.]

"What if you explained that the reason you're asking is to

compare her understanding of the priorities with yours to correct any misunderstanding?"

"It doesn't matter how I put it, if I ask her any question about what she's doing, it will sound like I'm questioning her judgment, and I'll just make an enemy." [Personal premise: Asking a person a question about what he's doing will make him angry at you.]

"There's no point in irritating her if you can help it. Would you get angry at her if she asked you why the reports are so important?" [Role reversal: a very effective tool.]

"No, I wouldn't. Why should I? It's a reasonable question." [Personal premises: I'm a reasonable person, and reasonable people don't get angry at reasonable questions.]

"Yes, it is. And isn't your question just as reasonable? I'm asking because if it is, she's not likely to get angry, either."

"Perhaps, but I'm not sure she's a reasonable person." [Personal premise: Unreasonable people could get angry at reasonable questions.]

"You consider yourself a reasonable person. Are you going to be guided by what's reasonable or by another person's possibly getting unreasonably angry?"

"Okay, I'll talk to her and ask her all the right questions. I'm not looking forward to it, but I've got to do the reasonable thing."

Discovering Your Own Personal Premises

Behind our reactions are personal premises. Some of these are true and some false. Without even being aware of what our personal premises are, we unconsciously reason from these premises to arrive at the reactions we give. Becoming conscious of your personal premises means understanding yourself, knowing why you do the things you do. You can then improve your behavior by exchanging your false premises for true ones.

We all operate on logic. Only the premises are different. Even the impulsive individual comes to the logical conclusion to act impulsively based on such premises as, *Go after the pleasure and avoid the pain that's here now; the future will take care of itself.* If a paranoid psychotic starts with the false premise that there are enemies all around trying to kill him, he could reason logically that he should shoot everyone near him. If the premises were true, a sane person might do the same thing.

Premises interact with each other. A person might put off buying a new car to replace his old one, which still runs but looks sloppy and needs repairs. He doesn't have the cash to pay for the new car, and he holds the premise *Don't borrow*. However, he might borrow if his wife or child needed an operation, because he has a still stronger premise that says, *Do anything to keep your family healthy*.

Suppose a person on his way out of a restaurant pockets the extra change he sees the cashier give him by mistake. However, he refuses to use someone else's commutation ticket on the train. What premise guides him? It can't be *Don't steal train rides, but steal excess change in restaurants*, because personal premises are generally not that narrow. However, it could be Steal only when you're sure you can get away with it. He could be sure with the change but not with the train ride.

You could find searching for your own personal premises exciting, highly rewarding, and perhaps upsetting. At times, you might not like what you see, but then you could change the premises you don't like if you want to.

A good way to do this is to ask yourself why did you decide the particular way you did where there were other options you could have chosen. Then think of other similar situations where you had to make the same kind of decision. Then try to think of a premise that would cause you to reason to that decision.

Check it out by asking yourself if that premise seems to explain your decisions in still other situations where it should apply.

People vary in how deeply they can delve into themselves to find their premises. However, some premises are so deeply held that it takes a counselor or psychotherapist to unearth them and get the individual to face them.

Suppose a woman with a teenaged son and daughter suddenly realizes that she has spent much more time talking to her son than to her daughter about what career to pursue. This occurs to her one day when her son says to her, "Listen, Mom, stop pestering me about taking something practical in college. I'm not interested in engineering or accounting. I want to be a journalist. Go bother Margaret [his sister] for a change."

The woman wonders why she concentrates on her son. She looks for her premises. One premise seems to be: *The man is responsible for making the money and the woman for making the home and raising the children.* This makes her wonder how liberated she really is even though she's sympathetic to the women's movement.

Has she done anything else that supports that premise? Well, she hasn't worked at a job since she got married. And she's more concerned about her son's grades in school than about her daughter's. Also, she talks much more to her daughter than to her son about planning meals and shopping. From her suggestion to her son that he go into engineering or accounting, she seems to be operating on the premise *Your security [which to her means success] in a career depends on whether there is a big demand in the society for people in the occupation you choose, rather than on whether you have talent for and are interested in your occupation.*

Has she done anything else that supports that premise? She remembers that when her husband wanted to leave his secure position as an underwriter for a large insurance company in order to become an insurance salesman on a commission basis, she encouraged him to stay in underwriting. Yet he might have been better at selling and enjoyed it more.

Finding Out and Dealing with Another's Personal Premises

To persuade the other person, you may have to find out what personal premises are supporting his objection. Why does he believe his objection is so? You have to listen carefully for anything that sounds like a personal premise, and separate these from premises that belong to the particular situation.

Generally, the kind of personal premise I'm talking about here is a broad generalization that applies to many situations and reflects a personal attitude or belief. The situational premise is one that applies only to the particular idea you're discussing.

If a person's premise for resisting a project you suggest is that there isn't enough money available, he's arguing on the basis of something in the specific situation. Let's call this basis (not enough money, in this case) a situational premise. But if he argues on the basis of some generalization that applies to this case but also to a lot of other cases, he's arguing on the basis of a personal premise. Such a premise might be: *When your employee is working far away from you, things are likely to go wrong because you can't supervise him closely enough.* With the situational premise, he's talking about only this situation. With the personal premise, he's really talking about all such situations.

Often, he'll first give a situational premise as the basis. You don't know at this point whether there is a personal premise behind it. You have to dig further to find out. Let's listen to the conversation.

"Did you get a chance to read my project proposal?"

"Yes, I did. It sounds good but we just don't have the money available." (Situational premise.)

"I guess we couldn't add another project. What I was wondering is, could we do this project now in place of one of our less promising projects? This project could bring us a much higher return than some others. The possibilities are really great here."

"I don't know. I'm not sure we have the people who could handle this kind of project. It takes special abilities." (Situational premise.)

"That's true, but why wouldn't Larry and Liz be just right for this? They both have the particular expertise required, and years of experience in related types of projects."

"But this project would be carried out at a distant location. They'd have to make a lot of decisions on their own. I'm not sure they're able to do that well enough." (Situational premise.)

"They'd certainly have to do that. But what makes you doubt that they can? They've done it successfully in previous jobs they've had."

"Well, I don't know if the previous jobs involved anything exactly like this project. Things could get out of hand. They wouldn't be able to consult with me about a lot of on-the-spot decisions. It's better to have closer control. Otherwise, things could go wrong. That kind of thing always makes me uneasy." (Personal premise: If I don't supervise closely, something will go wrong.)

Finally, the personal premise comes out. The individual operating on this premise is not necessarily aware that he holds this as a personal premise. It may feel to him as though he just thinks it for this particular case. But he seems to have some uneasiness about it since he worked his way gradually to mentioning it.

Objections based on broad personal premises are harder to deal with than are objections that arise from the situation. A broad personal premise influences so much of a person's behavior that giving up the premise is too threatening to him. Getting a person to give up a broad personal premise is beyond the scope of a business discussion. Dislodging personal premises that lead him to act in ways that hurt him often requires skilled counseling or therapy.

In selling your idea, when you encounter the personal premise behind an objection, it's better to introduce a compromise that reduces the conflict between your idea and his premise. Let's pick up the conversation from where it left off. The other person has just revealed his personal premise.

"We do want to keep in close touch with what they're doing. What if we arrange for them to consult with you by phone on what problems they're encountering and how they handled or plan to handle them? In that way you could correct anything wrong that they're doing, and you'd be able to tell how well they can do on their own. If they're consistently right in what they're doing, and as they learn more, you can if you wish reduce the frequency of their consulting with you. Their past performance makes me confident that they'll bring in the big gains that can be had from this project."

"Well, let me think about it. But if we go ahead with it, we'd have to make sure they understand they're to call whenever they have any question at all, no matter how small."

If you attack the personal premise head-on, you aren't likely to make much headway. It might sound something like this:

"We don't want anything to go wrong, but what makes you think it will, considering their good experience?"

"Something might come up that they haven't had any experience with. And they might mess it up in a costly way. I just feel better if I can watch things closely."

"It's true something new to them might happen. But as they were gaining experience, something must have come up every so often that they had no experience with. They had to use their judgment. And they've generally come out right."

"It's still better if they have both their judgment and mine. It greatly reduces the chance of something going wrong."

"Sure it does. But how can you be everywhere at once? You have to be doing the long-range planning and making the bigger decisions."

"I've managed pretty well so far."

"Yes, you have. But how are you going to develop your employees, give them confidence in their own problem-solving and decision-making, if you watch them so closely?"

"My employees are damn good. I'll match them against anyone else's."

People are likely to fight to hold on to their personal premises, particularly the broad ones. They'll resist giving them up in any way that suits them. They might use anger, rationalizations, withdrawal, or any other means. You'll find it much easier to make progress through accommodation.

‖ 7 ‖ Making a Convincing Case

Too Many Predictions
Based on Too Little Evidence

"Say, Jane, I hear you're looking for solid evidence that'll convince your boss that your idea will work. Well, there's this terrific tea-leaf reader I know. Try your idea on her. If she says it'll work, you can use what she says as evidence to convince your boss."

"He hates tea. He's big on coffee. Can she do anything with that?"

"She's on shaky grounds with coffee. It might be the way she grinds up the beans."

"How's she with a crystal ball?"

"Never uses it. Says the glare bothers her eyes."

"Has she tried sunglasses?"

"Well, listen, what if I told you I know a place where they tried your idea and it worked real well. Lowered their costs by twenty percent."

"My boss is funny that way. That's the kind of thing he really goes for."

You need evidence to enlist the other person's drive toward reasonableness. If you don't have evidence, the other person may very well feel that you're just being wishful. He might then allow his natural resistance free rein. But when you present evidence, he becomes anxious that if he doesn't consider your evidence reasonably, he will lose.

Like the tea-leaf reader, many of us make a number of predictions with more confidence than our evidence justifies. Some people claim that crime will go down with improved economic opportunity while others opt for stricter laws and law enforcement. There are those who cry out for us to get back to basics in education, and those who want to get still more innovative. One group wants to arm further, and another to disarm. All of these people are convinced they're right, mostly based on their personal premises, but seldom does anyone have enough evidence to convince others.

The use of computers to project what will happen makes the predicting look foolproof. How can things go wrong if the computer says so? But these computer projections are based on sets of assumptions. These assumptions are included in the facts and reasoning that are fed into the computer. The assumptions might be that certain things will remain the same, other things will change to particular extents, and still others that you are not taking into account will not affect the situation. There is only a certain probability that these assumptions are correct, and therefore that the prediction is correct.

The relationship between the person and the computer comes down to this: The person asks the question; he tells the computer what facts to use; he instructs the computer in how to reason from the facts to the answer; then he asks for the answer. This means that we can make many more predictions about many more happenings much sooner. But the rightness of the predictions depends on what evidence and what logic the person uses in deciding what to tell the computer.

The computer does fill an emotional need, too. It gives us someone to blame. But someday a sympathetic scientist will teach the computer how to defend itself from unfair criticism. But if the scientist teaches it wrongly, we could get defensive computers. Then we'll just be making electronic people.

How Evidence Persuades

The world of nature is an orderly place. There are rules covering everything. These rules tell us what to expect. We don't make these rules; we just discover them and use them. Down through the ages we've discovered many rules, but these are only a small portion of nature's rule book. Countless more rules are waiting to be discovered.

We discover these rules by observing the same situations over and over. Therefore, all rules are based on past experience. If you run more electricity through a wire than it can carry, it heats up, glows, and burns up. We also learn that in order for something to burn up, there must be oxygen present. Edison put these two rules together and produced the light bulb. He took a wire that could carry only a little electricity, so that the wire glowed to produce light without requiring a great deal of electric current. And to keep the wire glowing, he encased it in a glass container and removed all the oxygen from this container so that the wire wouldn't burn up.

These rules of nature work every time. Whenever you raise the temperature of any gas it expands. And its pressure against whatever it's next to goes up. We use this pressure to run automobile and jet-plane engines.

However, predicting *individual human behavior* is largely a matter of probabilities. We haven't discovered enough rules of nature to be sure of our predictions about how people will react. We know in general that people move toward rewards and away from the things that hurt them. But how these rewards and hurts are valued varies with the individual. For one person the pay is the primary incentive for working. For another, it's his interest in the job. We can predict the behavior of groups at a higher probability than for individuals, but we're still dealing in probabilities.

We have to make predictions continually. Every decision we make is based on a prediction. We might be predicting which marketing approach will turn out best for particular products, how well an individual will perform if promoted, or how much we'll be pleased by the TV program we turn on.

We make our predictions based on what evidence we can gather. The two main types of evidence for predicting are: a) reasoning from a rule of nature to what will happen; and b) past experience, *our own or others'*, with a situation similar to the one we're predicting about.

Rules of nature provide the most reliable evidence since they always work. If we're planning a vacation at the seashore, we can predict for sure that we'll have ocean breezes. Since earth and water heat up at different rates during the day and cool down at different rates at night, a breeze blows one way or the other. Since hot air rises, the breeze blows from the cooler side to fill the vacuum under the warmer air of the other side.

Similarly, you can predict that mold will develop on fruit, that the moving parts of any equipment will wear out at their points of contact, and that a wound in a normal human body will heal.

We discover a rule of nature from repeated observations that the same cause always produces the same effect. The maximum load that a steel wire of a certain thickness can hold is a thousand pounds. Above this load it always breaks. The rule is solid evidence for predicting what will happen, and it comes from past experience.

We also develop rules from the repeated observations we make informally as part of our everyday experience. These rules provide good evidence for selling our prediction when these rules are part of the common experience. While everyone knows them, they're not based on scientific inquiry.

Some examples of such rules are: Trains and highways are crowded at rush hour; people behave consistently in some ways so that we can characterize them as prompt, big spenders, conscientious, excitable, cautious; and the same thing won't please everyone.

Past experience can be useful evidence even when we don't know all the rules covering the situation. Since the world is orderly, if one thing caused another before, it will do so again. We just can't be as sure because, without knowing the rules, we don't know what the effects are of the differences between the past situation and the one we're predicting about. When you have a lot of things happening in the same situation, there's bound to be something different in the situation each time it occurs. Even when we know what the difference is, we may not know its effect. We don't know the rule that covers it. Sometimes whatever differences are there matter, and sometimes they don't.

If the idea we're trying to sell were successful 80 percent of the time, it means that there's an 80 percent chance that it will succeed this time. Whatever differences occurred caused failure 20 percent of the time. Whether this chance is worth taking depends on the return on investment we're expecting if it succeeds. If that return is 50 percent, then the average return on repeated use of this idea, which succeeds four out of five times, is 40 percent, which is a good return on investment. This is strong evidence for the idea, and can be used in response to an objection that the idea is too risky.

The decision to buy an idea should depend both on the chance that the idea will succeed and the rate of return if it does. You have to first set the minimum average return that's acceptable. Then calculate the average return by multiplying the return if it succeeds by the probability that it will, to see if this average return exceeds your minimum acceptable one.

You have to make sure that you use your evidence soundly, whether to support your idea or to oppose an objection. If at any point the other person finds that your evidence doesn't justify what you're claiming, you'll lose credibility. Your whole presentation will become suspect.

Three things to check in evidence that's based on past experience only are:

1. How many cases do you have where your idea was used, and of these, how many were successful?

2. How similar are the situations where your idea was previously used to the situation where you want to use it now?

3. How similar are the objectives where your idea was previously used to your objective in the present situation? (If the objectives were different, what was successful then might not be considered successful now.)

You can use these three questions to evaluate not only the evidence for your idea but also the other person's evidence for his objections. When the other person objects to some part of your idea that you haven't yet explained to him, he's likely to be basing his objection on his past experience with an idea that's somewhat similar to yours and used in somewhat similar situations. Yet there might be critical differences in both the idea and the situations.

In using evidence to support your idea, even if you have only one case where your idea was used before, or there were some differences in the idea or in the situation, your evidence could still be useful. It's just *less* useful. And if the payoff is high enough, that evidence may be good enough.

You sell a product that's presently bought seventy-five percent by men and twenty-five percent by women. You've advertised only three times using the same ad, all in the same men's magazine, at four-month intervals, and all the ads paid off. You can predict with good confidence that although it is now four months after your last ad, so that times are a little different, your next ad will be successful. You can predict success with progressively less confidence if you switch to another men's magazine, if you use a women's magazine, or if you change the ad.

You can look for additional evidence in others' experiences. Did someone with a similar product advertise in one of these magazines? If so, how similar was his ad, and how successful? Then you estimate from the evidence the confidence you can have in predicting. Is the chance excellent, good, fair, or poor? The next question is, what confidence do you have that you'll get back the minimum return you need to justify the ad? If the return you got before was way above this minimum, you might need only a good or fair, or sometimes even a poor, level of confidence that you'll get back this minimum.

Remember, if there's only a fifty percent chance of gaining success in achieving something, but if you do you'll get back three times your investment, it's worth doing. It's not the risk alone that determines if a venture is worthwhile, but whether the payoff justifies the risk.

When the other person raises the objection that your idea is too risky, one important question to ask is, why does he consider your idea too risky considering the size of the payoff if the idea succeeds? You want also to find out whether he is overestimating the risk, by finding out what he bases his estimate on.

If you don't have evidence, the conversation can very easily slide into a yes-it-is, no-it-isn't exchange. Each person feels free to say something is so without having evidence for it since the other person has no evidence against it. Listen to this.

"We're spending too much money on the packaging of our product to make sure it doesn't break. Right now we could probably drop it from a ten-story building and there'd be no damage. We don't need that much protection."

"We don't have that much protection. Packages get rough handling by shippers. We can't afford breakage. It's too expensive. And we annoy the customers."

"We could cut the packaging down without getting more breakage. We have way more packaging than we need. It's like carrying too much insurance."

"What we've got is just right. I don't want to look for trouble. The customers are happy and I'm happy."

"But we're throwing away profit for nothing. You would be still happier with more profit, wouldn't you?"

"Sure, but we'd wind up with less profit. We'd lose product and business."

"No, we wouldn't."

"Yes, we would."

The person who suggested reducing the packaging should have first gathered evidence by: Calculating the possible savings from reduced packaging; testing this reduced packaging through simulated rough handling; estimating the amount of breakage that's likely to occur; and figuring out whether the savings in packaging would justify the estimated breakage and reshipping costs, and whatever customer irritation would occur.

Suppose a manager in sales plans to persuade the vice-president of sales to stop the new practice of hiring less qualified technical service people and sending them into the field with less training, in order to save on salary costs. The vice-president of sales has responsibility for both sales and technical service. The manager's research into the problem reveals that for twenty percent of the customer complaints that the three most recently hired technical service representatives are sent to customers to deal with, the reps can't find what's causing the problem. They don't know how to troubleshoot well enough. As a result, another more skilled technical service person has to be sent out. The manager feels this will lead to a loss of business, as well as increase the cost of technical service.

The manager needs evidence both to support her idea and to counter the vice-president's objections to it.

Now the manager has to anticipate as many objections as she can, and develop the evidence against them. Let's suppose she anticipates the following objections and then gathers the following evidence to be prepared for them.

1. ANTICIPATED OBJECTION: I'd rather put the money saved on salaries into making sales, by hiring another salesperson.

Counterevidence: After subtracting the cost of the replacement calls for three technical service reps, we'd hardly have anything left to pay for a salesperson.

2. ANTICIPATED OBJECTION: It's not any ineffectiveness on the part of our service representatives that's causing the trouble. It's that customers are cutting corners on the quality of their people who use our products. As a result, they're getting more problems and more of these are difficult.

Counterevidence: The newer service representatives have less technical background and are given less training. A survey of the problems that customers present shows no change in the number or difficulty of the problems. Our skilled reps can handle them as well as they always have. Furthermore, even if it were true that the customers' people who use our products are less capable and are causing more problems, that's all the more reason for our people to all be highly competent.

3. ANTICIPATED OBJECTION: Even if the first visit is ineffective and we have to send someone more skilled, the customer is

pleased by our prompt response and our willingness to pursue his problems with a more capable representative.

Counterevidence: The fact is, if the first visit is not effective, the customer has to live longer with the problem. This costs him more. And a third of the customers who received ineffective first visits complained about this. They want a competent service rep on the first visit.

4. ANTICIPATED OBJECTION: Our competition isn't doing any better than we are.

Counterevidence: I talked to a sample of our salespeople about this, and on the average they told me that where our customers used more than one supplier of our kind of products, twenty-five percent of the buyers pointed out, without being asked, that they had better technical service from our competitors.

5. ANTICIPATED OBJECTION: The new less qualified reps will gradually improve with experience, and become as good as the old reps.

Counterevidence: Some will, and some won't be able to over-some their lack of technical background and the frustration of having twenty percent failures in handling customer problems. But even for those who do, any loss of business that occurs because of ineffective first visits would be so much more than the savings in salaries that the risk isn't worth taking.

Now that the manager has gathered this evidence, she can't just bounce it back as the objections are thrown at her. She'd irritate the vice-president by making him lose face. The manager has to use the evidence in a gentle, supportive, inquiring way. Let's watch her do this as she starts the conversation with a bottom-line opening.

"I did some research into how well we're doing in hiring

bright people with no technical background at a lower salary, and shortening their training period. I was surprised to find it's not working out as well as we hoped. We're likely to lose more in sales than we'll gain in cost cutting. I think we ought to go back to hiring technical people and giving them more training."

"We've got to make it work. With business harder to get, we need another salesperson badly but I haven't got the budget for it. By cutting costs in technical service, we'll be able to hire one."

"The way things are another salesperson could make a lot of difference. But what if we didn't save near as much as we thought we would? Let me share with you what I discovered. The three new tech service reps can't handle the problems for twenty percent of their calls. A more skilled rep has to be called in. This is a waste of the new reps' time because they don't realize they can't handle it until after they've made the call and looked into the problem. Calling in a skilled rep for twenty percent of each of three new reps' calls means we're using up an extra sixty percent of a skilled rep's time. This almost washes out any savings we'd make."

"The trouble is, the customers are bringing a lot of the problems on themselves. They're cutting corners on the quality and training of their people. So they make more mistakes with more complications, and then we have to straighten things out. With more complicated problems, they've got to give our new people a little more time so that they can handle the problems without calling in the more experienced reps."

"That makes sense and they probably are doing what cost cutting they can. But if the effects of the cost cutting were showing, wouldn't we expect our skilled reps to be having a harder time than before? I checked with them and they say not, it's still pretty much the same old problems."

"You know our old-time skilled reps. They don't like to admit that anything fazes them. Anyway, your customers can't complain about promptness. Our reps are there right after the customer calls. So even when we have to send in a skilled rep to replace a new one, at least the customer sees how quickly we respond and how interested we are."

"Oh, we're right there, all right. We don't delay. But how would we feel if we had to wait longer for our problem to get solved because the first rep our supplier sent couldn't handle it? Probably about the same as most of our customers do. About a third of them complained about it to our salespeople, according to what they told me. So maybe another third felt irritated but didn't bother to complain."

"Things are damn tough. Everybody's got to be cutting costs. So our competition can't be doing any better than we are."

"They're probably cutting wherever they can. But listen to what I found out, because it really bothers me. I talked to a number of the salespeople to see if they were getting any flak about our technical service. They told me that about a quarter of their customers who were buying our kind of product from both us and another supplier brought up on their own that they're getting better technical service from the other supplier. So probably still another quarter of the customers feels the same way but didn't bring it up. I wish I knew what they're doing, because it doesn't seem to be hurting them."

"You know the salespeople. They exaggerate some. They want us to make it easy for them. We just have to give the new reps a little time. They'll improve with experience and become as good as the old reps."

"You're right, some will. But how many of them won't be able to overcome their lack of technical background, and their frustration at failing with twenty percent of their customers' problems? And the bottom-line question is, does the very small saving justify the very real risk of losing some business? It seems to me that if just one buyer got annoyed and cut us out, or even cut down our share, it would wash out any saving we might make."

"I can see you're really on top of this thing. If you're convinced that we should go back to our old standards for technical service reps, okay, let's do it. We can't afford to lose any business."

The More Evidence You Have, the Lower the Risk Is

You're not likely to sell an idea if you don't have enough evidence that it will work. Any idea you suggest is competing with whatever is in place now, which the decision maker knows from experience works as well as it does. To that extent there's no risk. But if your evidence shows that your idea will work still better, a reasonable decision maker will buy your idea.

You don't need ironclad evidence. Criminal court standards are not used. In the criminal court contest, the prosecution has to supply enough evidence to make the accused look guilty beyond a reasonable doubt. The defense tries to undermine this evidence enough to maintain a reasonable doubt. But in civil court, where one party sues another, the decision depends on which side has the strongest evidence. There still can be reasonable doubt.

The same is true in selling an idea. You don't need to eliminate reasonable doubt. What you have to do is have enough evidence to bring the risk down to where it's worth taking.

Try to get an extra margin of evidence. How much extra you need depends on how open-minded the decision maker is, and how willing to take risks. Balance the cost of getting the extra evidence against what it adds in persuasive strength.

Some evidence you can get from your own experience and some by just making phone calls to people who have had experience with an idea like yours. Move from the easiest-to-consult records and literature to the more difficult. Leave making surveys and doing experiments for last.

The evidence you gather may very well take care of all the objections. However, if some objections get by you and remain standing, the benefits may still outweigh the objections. But since the standing objections either raise the risk or lower the payoff, the risk from other sources has to be lower. This is why any extra margin of evidence is handy to have.

You have to be careful that your evidence justifies the buying of your idea. For your evidence affects your credibility in general as well as the sale of this idea. If your evidence isn't good enough to sell your idea, hold back on expressing your enthusiasm and go after more evidence. Otherwise, your lowered credibility will diminish your chances with future ideas.

If you present an idea with solid evidence and you don't sell it, it doesn't necessarily mean you haven't made progress. The other person may conceal some things that are in the way at that time; or perhaps his resistance to others' ideas is too high at the moment; or he may be experiencing some stress that's preventing an objective evaluation. Still, the idea may percolate within him so that the next time you try to sell it, he's more responsive; or he may ask you more about it at a later time.

‖ 8 ‖ Getting Through the Resistance Barrier

**Everyone Has Resistance
But We Don't See Our Own**

"I've come to realize that we all have some resistance to other people's ideas. Someone alerted me to this and I've been watching myself and others. It took me a while to see it."

"Well, I don't. That's one thing I pride myself on. I don't care whose idea it is. If it's good, I'll buy it. I go strictly by the facts."

"Here you are resisting this very idea I just told you, that we all have resistance—you, me, everybody."

"I'm not resisting anything. If I disagree with you, you call it resistance."

"It's because you disagreed so fast without even thinking about it. I told you that it took me a while to see it, but you didn't ask me a single question."

"I have thought about it. I'm always amazed about how people's minds are made up, closed to ideas you try to give them."

"And you feel that you're the world class open-minded exception?"

"I think being open-minded is rare, and I'm one of the rare ones."

"All those people you meet who are closed to others' ideas, do you think that they see themselves as closed? Or do they consider themselves open-minded?"

"Sure, they consider themselves open-minded. I never heard anyone say he was closed to other people's ideas. People don't see themselves as they really are."

"Then how do you know that you're not sometimes closed but think you're being open? Like now, for example."

"I just do. I know myself."

"Is that the kind of answer anyone who's resisting might give?"

"Listen, if I weren't so open-minded, I wouldn't have put up with this conversation so long. I've got to go see Charlie now about an idea I have that would benefit both of us. See you later."

"Be ready for his resistance."

To some extent, we all have resistance to others' ideas. This resistance is unreasonable in that it has little to do with whether anything's wrong with the idea. And it's this unreasonableness that prevents us from seeing our own resistance.

Since we have a strong need to feel and appear reasonable, we don't face our own resistance. We try to make the resistance look reasonable to ourselves and others. We generally do this by rationalizing.

Rationalizing is logical lying. You disguise the lie by developing a logical argument to support it. It's more subtle than a flat lie. Generally, you design it to deceive yourself as well as the other person, so the error has to be a little hard to see right off. With a flat lie you know you're lying.

Skillful rationalizing requires that you make your factual errors and the holes in your logic as small as you can get by with. You have to be both logical and creative to do this well. And doing it well is important for both your comfort and your image. For if your distortions are obvious, you won't fool yourself; and the other person is likely to feel that you either don't think he's bright or else don't care what he thinks.

For your rationalizing to get by, the other person has to want to believe. If he's skeptical, he's likely to ask enough good questions to expose your little deception. But if he doesn't care or doesn't want to embarrass you, he'll go along.

Listen to a skeptical wife questioning her husband's rationalizing.

"Why did you buy a new set of tools, and such expensive ones? You already have all these tools."

"Well, there's something about the feel of better quality tools that makes you work better. Take those pliers. They're more versatile. You can do more things with them."

"But you do so little work around the house as it is. It takes so long to get you to make a repair."

"That's just it. With these fine, high-quality tools, I'll be more motivated to use them."

"But all these things that you bought—the hammer, pliers, wrench, and screwdrivers in assorted sizes—don't the ones you have work well? You never complain about them."

"Well, they're all right. But they're getting a little worn. I could take longer with them, and you don't do as good a job."

"Worn? How do a hammer, plier, and the other things get worn, especially when you use them so little? Can't you drive a nail in with a worn hammer, and turn a screw with a worn screwdriver, especially with the little wear your tools have?"

"Okay, okay, you've made your point. I guess maybe I indulged myself a bit. I'll take them back."

Why People
Resist Others' Ideas

When you try to sell an idea to someone, you disturb him in a number of ways. For one thing, you introduce a new way of handling a particular kind of situation when he already has a way comfortably in place. A new way means risk that it won't work as well as the old way does. On the other hand, it might work better. Automatically you've placed him in the uncomfortable position of being uncertain about what to do. So initially he resists even considering your idea in order to avoid becoming involved and having to decide.

He knows that as soon as he starts to consider your idea, he'll be caught up in chasing and fitting together information in order to grasp the significance of your idea. For the more information he gets, the better he understands the risk. But he'd rather not have the mental and emotional turbulence that comes from the uncertainty.

Another cause of his resistance is his insecurity. Most of us have some insecurity. We wonder about how good we are socially, mentally, morally, physically, sexually. There's no absolute standard for this so we compare ourselves to others, and also get feedback from them.

If someone comes to us with a good idea, we wonder why we didn't think of it and what that signifies about us. We feel still worse when the idea comes from someone with less knowledge and experience than we have. Similarly, when we try to sell our idea to another person, he's likely to look for things wrong with it so that he can reject it. His effort to do this depends on how insecure he is.

The competitiveness most of us have also contributes to our resistance. We compete in the family, in school, on the job, in sports, and socially. We compete with predatory animals for our livestock, with insects for our crops, and with bacteria and viruses for our bodies. Nations, schools, businesses, clubs, all compete with each other.

Insecurity and competitiveness reinforce each other. Insecurity drives us to go after more than we need. This heightens our competitiveness. Furthermore, since we compare ourselves to others in order to get some measure of ourselves, surpassing others may enlarge our self-image. Losing to them can diminish it, making us feel less secure.

When you try to sell someone your idea, he feels in competition with you. Whose idea will be used, his or yours? If it's his, he wins, and feels bigger for it. This motivates him to look for something wrong with yours.

When buying your idea means making a change, the other person's natural resistance to change adds to his resistance to your idea. Resistance to change is built into us in that to do something new we first have to learn it. This means going up a learning curve, which shows how a person's learning something increases with his repeating it.

Each time we repeat it, we learn more of it, until we've learned it all. This means that in order to sell an idea we have to wait until the other person learns it, which is a gradual process. Learning your idea can't be rushed. Learning through repetition is the way the brain is built to work, whether it be the brain of a worm, a frog, a cat, or a person. The gradualness of our learning an idea can be viewed as resulting from a natural resistance, comparable to a wire's resistance to the electric current that flows through it.

Depending on how complex the idea is, learning it may take many repetitions or none, which can mean weeks or minutes. The other person has to absorb what you want to do, what the benefits are, what other effects will occur, how others will react, what risks he incurs, and all the other moving parts. He has to develop an easy understanding of how these moving parts affect each other. And he has to get used to the idea, become emotionally comfortable with it.

We live by habits. Learning something new means giving up an old habit for a new one. The gradualness helps us to survive by preventing us from adopting ideas rashly, even though this holds up good ideas.

You have to be patient in selling your ideas in order to accommodate for the resistance that will inevitably be there. It's easy to forget that you learned and got used to your own idea while developing it. And no matter how clearly you present the information, the other person still has to learn it both on thinking and on feeling levels. She has to go through enough layers of understanding so that her grasp of your idea is deep enough for her to feel at ease with it.

Her talking about your idea gives her this deeper understanding much more so than your talking does. While she talks about it, she's getting a feel of it; she's trying it on. Your questions to her also prod her to do this. When she's talking, be careful not to disturb this valuable learning activity. Don't interrupt her. Don't try to say it better than she does. And don't try to get her to think about it in a different sequence of thoughts. She has her own way. Let her follow it.

The Ways People Resist

There are a number of ways of resisting, some more subtle than others. Some people have mastered them all and use them with great finesse. Other people are content with using just a few over and over. Perhaps they're less concerned with hiding their resistance.

Nit-picking is one way of resisting. The person resisting magnifies small problems, presenting them as huge barriers when actually they should be considered little issues to be resolved after the idea is bought. He does this to prevent the discussion from getting anywhere. When the other person picks a nit, you might reply with: "That is something to consider. Would it be all right with you if I noted it down for us to take up after we've developed the whole picture of how this idea would work? In doing this, a solution to that problem might emerge." In general, you have to adjust your response to the person you're dealing with, and to your relationship with him.

Changing the subject is another way of resisting. The person resisting may go off on irrelevancies, or she may change the subject altogether by saying, "By the way, what do you think of such and such?" You can reply with: "I'm interested in talking to you about that. Do you want, though, to finish with our original topic first? It seems to me we ought to resolve that."

When the other person holds back on giving you information, he's probably resisting. He might not answer your questions fully, or may explain something meagerly. You may find yourself asking a lot of extra questions that shouldn't be necessary. To get him to be more cooperative, you could say: "I could be wrong but it seems to me that you don't much feel like talking about this." This should clear the air, and lead to the other person's either cooperating or ending the conversation.

Excessive tuning out is another sign of resistance. The other person doesn't link up with your thinking. She keeps asking you to repeat something, or she responds in a way that shows she hasn't heard what you said. At some point you might say: "You seem to have other things on your mind." She's likely then to either listen more closely or put off the conversation for another time. In any case, you're better off than trying to talk at her when she's not with you.

One more sign of resistance is the other person's becoming impatient or irritable. You might then comment; "You seem impatient." Again, he might calm down and ask you to go on, or he might stop the discussion. Either result is better than trying to sell your idea when he doesn't want to listen.

The conversation below is unreal, but it shows what could happen if people expressed some of the feelings caused by their resistance to others' ideas:

"I'd like to propose to you a great idea you're suggesting."

"I like it already."

"I haven't told it to you yet."

"But it's mine, isn't it?"

"Yes, and that's why it's so good."

"I can hardly wait to hear it."

"You're thinking that if we reinstated that recruiting procedure that didn't work last year, we'd come out way ahead. Things weren't right for it then, but they're just right now."

"I'm glad you like my idea."

"Of course I do. If it weren't your idea, it wouldn't work."

"Tell me more about my idea so I'll know how it'll work."

A subtle sign of resistance is the use of objections rather than questions. When the other person makes a positive assertion that people will resent your idea, he's resisting. He isn't motivated to try to make your idea work. If he were motivated, he would ask questions rather than object. He might ask you how you think people will react, or if you think people would resent your idea. He would want to use your idea and would ask questions to see if you have any way of handling the problems that come to his mind.

If he were open-minded, he would figure that since you proposed the idea, you've probably thought about the problems that the idea might cause and how to deal with them. And he would ask questions to find out what you would do about the concerns that come to his mind.

But if he's resisting and doesn't want your idea to work, he would thrust objections at you and then try to think of ways to knock down your answers. Usually, he isn't even aware that he's resisting. He feels that his thrusts and knockdowns are logical ways of evaluating your idea.

You might be thinking now that the other person could just be playing the devil's advocate as a way of testing the idea. But isn't it more productive to test an idea by having both people look for ways to deal with all the problems that both of them can think of, than to have just one person bring up problems and the other deal with them? The devil would certainly resist a good idea, and his advocate would want to be devilish.

Since an objection represents resistance that is at least partly unreasonable, don't argue against it. Instead, ask for the reasoning behind it, or for the specifics or quantities, or ask whether something you have in mind would take care of the objection.

People resist also by making reasoning errors. We're too practiced in reasoning to make them by accident. We've been reasoning all our lives and it's not that difficult. In fact, it's harder to contrive a reasoning error that looks innocently made than to reason correctly, which is second nature. When someone makes a reasoning error, it means that he doesn't want to do the logical thing.

Listen to this and see if you think it's so easy to make reasoning errors.

"Bill, why don't you go in for a swim? You'll cool off."

"The way the water is polluted these days, I don't like to take a chance."

"But this is a community swimming pool. It's cleaned and chlorinated."

"That's what they tell you but I know a guy who went swimming in a pool like this, and the next day he came down with an infection. Some kind of virus."

"How do you know he got the virus from the pool?"

"Because that's the only place where he went swimming during the previous two weeks."

"Maybe he caught the virus from someone."

"No, it was the pool. Everyone knows that polluted swimming pools cause infections."

"What makes you think that the pool was polluted?"

"He caught a virus, didn't he?"

You've got to be mentally agile and highly motivated to reason with so many illogical twists. It's much easier to reason correctly because it's natural. Perhaps this person is chronically afraid that he'll get sick but doesn't want to admit it. So he has to keep developing rationalizations for avoiding the many things that threaten him.

Resistance to Specific Ideas

Resistance to others' ideas has two parts. One is the resistance just because the idea comes from someone else; and the other is resistance because the specific idea goes against a particular personal premise that influences the individual more than the idea's benefits do. When you're selling your idea, you have to get through both of these resistances as well as deal with the logical objections.

Suppose you're trying to persuade a manager to reduce his supervisory span. He has too many people reporting to him and therefore can't give enough attention to any of them. He can't supervise in depth because he can't gain a full ongoing understanding of each person's needs and problems. Nor can he develop the people under him. You suggest reorganizing so that some of his people and their jobs come under another manager.

He resists the idea not only because it comes from you, rather than from himself, but also because it goes against a personal premise of his as follows: *The more people you have under you, the more powerful and secure you are.* This premise carries more weight with him than does the idea's benefit that he'll be able to supervise better.

Suppose a high school girl wishes she could have a part in

the school play. Her mother urges her to try out. But the girl resists because she's governed by the following personal premise: *If I compete with others, I lose because there's always someone better than me; when I lose, I feel inadequate, which is painful.* She wants a part very much but her opposing personal premise is still stronger.

The other person generally hides the causes of his resistance because they're unreasonable. He is reluctant to reveal them to you unless he is open with you, and finds you generally understanding and supportive. Even then he will often conceal his personal premises.

It's not essential that you know the causes of the other person's resistance. What is important is that the other person become aware of them. You can get him to focus inwardly on the reasons for his resistance by suggesting that he may have other reasons for opposing your idea than those discussed. This causes him to look within himself for these other reasons. When he sees them, he is facing his unreasonableness, which may cause him to move back to the reasonable track. He's likely to do all this without telling you what went on in his mind. It doesn't matter. You've made him reasonable again, which means you can resume persuading with logic.

Reducing Resistance by Asking About Objections

You can reduce the other person's resistance by getting him to think reasonably. To accomplish this, in your reply to his objection: a) Set him an example of reasonableness; and b) get him to look reasonably at his own objection.

To set him an example, you have to deal reasonably yourself. This is more difficult than it seems. It looks easy because you probably think of yourself as being completely open-minded— one who is quite willing to listen and who goes by the facts.

But since we all think we're this way, and yet we all have resistance, we deal unreasonably without realizing it, unless we watch ourselves closely for signs of resistance. We have to make a conscious deliberate effort to listen openly and to ask questions, rather than develop an immediate negative reaction and argue back.

At the outset of the discussion, set your mind to resist your resistance. Resolve to avoid quick conclusions, to listen carefully, and to find out more about the other person's thinking. When the other person objects, make sure you look into his objection rather than reject it out of hand.

In order to deal with an objection effectively, you first have to understand the other person's train of thought that leads her to that objection. Why does she think that her objection is so? You need to find this out in order to see if her facts and reasoning are right.

One of the biggest hurdles in dealing with the other person's objections is his unreasonable resistance combined with his unwillingness to face it. His resistance can cause him to wishfully invent and distort facts as well as accept information that he wants to be so, and reject what he doesn't want to be true, without checking the information. His resistance can also cause him to reason wrongly from his facts to get the conclusion he wants.

If it were only a matter of your checking his facts and reasoning, it would still take patient, thoughtful questioning to uncover them. But there's another problem. His reluctance to face his resistance means that he *doesn't want* to uncover his facts and reasoning. For one thing, he doesn't want to give up his resistance. And for another, he doesn't want to appear unreasonable or incompetent, which could result from your questioning.

When your question is along the path of finding out why she thinks her objection is so, your inquiry could both worry and irritate her. Are you suggesting that her facts or reasoning could be wrong? Are you implying that she's incompetent, doesn't know what makes sense? She feels a little threatened. You have to allay her fears, and soothe her while asking your questions.

If someone feels highly secure in his self-image, he recognizes that he might think wishfully at times, and make errors. He welcomes having his thinking checked to make sure he's making the right decision. But most people are not that secure. So you have to incorporate reassurances in your questioning remarks.

To help maintain a mind-set of reasonableness and open-minded inquiring in both the other person and yourself, whenever he objects start your reply with an acknowledgment of something in his objection that you agree is true or at least worth considering. If he objects by saying, "That's too expensive," begin your reply with "It does cost a little more," or "We do have to watch the cost."

If he opposes by saying, "We tried that last year and it didn't work," you could start your reply with "It's true that it didn't work last year," or "We have to take last year's results into account." And if he resists with "The employees won't like this procedure," you could start with "Some of them might not," or "We have to be careful about their reaction."

Starting your reply with an acknowledgment establishes a tone of reasonableness. It shows you're listening to him, and willing to accept the part of his objection that makes sense to you even though it goes against your idea. This encourages him to do the same rather than adopt an adversary stance.

After your acknowledgment, you should continue reasonably in the same remark by asking a question to bring out the basis of the other person's objection. What facts and reasoning led him to his objection? At the same time, you have to tell what you're getting at with your question.

In asking a question and then explaining what you have in

mind in asking that question, you're displaying reasonableness. You want to know more about his objection to see how it affects your idea. Perhaps the other person's objection calls for changes in the idea, or makes it unacceptable. Or maybe the objection isn't true. Your telling why you're asking prevents an interrogation effect and makes the other person a partner in your thinking.

Let's put together the acknowledgment, question, and your reason for asking, all in one remark to form replies to objections. In the following replies we're assuming certain facts are so in order to explain the reason for the question.

The other person objects in reply to your suggestion:

"Sue is a natural leader and the best person for the supervisor opening. But Harry and Linda, who are competing for the job and have much more experience, would be very upset about being passed over by Sue. And all the others would resent her being made supervisor. She's younger and has less experience than most of them."

The questioning has to be done very supportively and sensitively. And because there's a risk that the questions may irritate him, you have to steel yourself with a reasonable assertiveness to ask the questions.

In forming your reply, you first have to acknowledge something in the objection that you agree with. You could agree that Harry and Linda would probably be upset about being passed over since they're competing for the job.

You could also agree that the others who are not competing are older and have more experience than Sue has. You have to aim your question at uncovering the logic behind the other part of his objection. There, he's saying that the others would resent Sue's being made supervisor because she's younger and less experienced.

But would they really resent it, since they gain in having the best person for their supervisor and they don't lose anything because they're not competing? Your reasoning leads you to the opposite conclusion from the manager's. How, then, did he arrive at his conclusion? Does he know something that you don't know? Or is there something wrong in your reasoning? Your question aims at finding out what leads him to his conclusion. And your reason for asking the question is your reasoning that leads you to come to the opposite conclusion. Your reasoning makes you wonder what his reasoning is that makes him come to his conclusion.

Suppose you ask the question, "Why do you think the others would resent it?" In the same remark, you would then add your reasoning that supports your conclusion that the employees wouldn't resent it. You could say, "They'll be getting the best supervisor, and they're not competing for the job, anyway." You may be wondering, why is it necessary to add the reasoning behind your question? Why can't you just ask your question without giving your reasoning? If you just ask your question—"Why do you think the others would resent it?"—the manager would just repeat what he said in his objection: "Because she's younger and has less experience than many of them."

The reason you get into this bind is that by asking the question without adding the reasoning behind it, you're not asking what you specifically mean to ask. This question without the reasoning added means, where would any resentment they experience come from? His response—"Because she's younger and has less experience than many of them,"—answers that question correctly, and you'd probably agree with it, but it's not the question you mean.

But when you add to your question your reasoning behind it, your question means what you want it to mean. Here, the question and reasoning together become: "Why do you think the others would resent it when they'd gain by getting the best person as supervisor, and they're not even competing for the job, anyway?"

With your reasoning added to your question, your question comes to mean, why do you think that their resentment outweighs their feeling that they've gained by getting the best person as supervisor, since they're not even competing for the job, anyway?

Now you might ask, why not put the question that way since that's what you really mean? The answer is, it would be fine if you did ask it that way. And if you can think quickly enough to work out the question that expresses just what you mean, by all means do it. But often we can't, so I'm suggesting an easier way. First, ask a broad question that at least covers what you mean even though your question could also mean other things. Then add what you had in mind to ask. By adding this, you narrow your question down to just exactly what you mean by it.

Putting together the acknowledgment, question, and the reasoning behind your question, you might reply:

"Sue is younger and less experienced than most of the others. Still, why would the ones other than Harry and Linda resent Sue's being made supervisor when they'd be getting a supervisor they'd feel happier about working for? None of them were in line for the job, anyway, so they're not being passed over. And we'd get the supervisor who's likely to make the unit the most productive."

In general, when you ask a question, tell the reasoning behind it if the reasoning isn't apparent. And when someone asks you a question, make sure you know the reasoning behind it before you answer it. If you do this, the answers are much more likely to fit the questions, and you and the other person will be talking mind to mind.

Let's look at another example. Suppose a woman is trying to persuade her husband to take a different kind of vacation this year. They'd be starting something new and might discover something more enjoyable.

He objects: "But we always have a good time at the cottage. We like the neighbors and the lake and the town. We might wind up much worse with something new. Let's stick with what we know is good."

She replies: [Acknowledgment.] "There is some risk that we could wind up worse off. [Question.] Wouldn't we likely do better rather than worse if we searched for a setting that would give us more of the things we enjoy than we have at the cottage? [Reasoning behind the question.] There's bound to be places that have still better fishing and swimming, still more interesting people, finer restaurants, and things that the cottage doesn't have at all like summer theater and scenic trails for walking. If we don't find a place that looks better, we'll go back to the cottage."

Suppose the sales manager of a medium-sized manufacturing company is trying to sell the president on having each new sales representative work for three weeks at the home office and plant before starting work in his territory. The sales manager opens with the bottom line.

"Our new sales representatives would make more sales if they'd spend three weeks here before they go to their territories. They'd work a couple of days in each department—production, customer service, shipping, credit, and the others. That way they could answer questions and think of alternatives much better. Their credibility would be higher."

"It would cost too much. With travel, food, lodging, and salaries, it just wouldn't pay off."

"It would cost a fair amount. Why do you think that doing this for three thousand dollars a sales rep couldn't pay off? If the sales reps sold only two percent more their first year, the program would pay for itself. And they might very well sell much more."

"How do you figure that?"

"The three-thousand-dollar cost is two percent of the one

hundred fifty thousand dollars in profit we usually net from a first-year sales rep. And if the program increases each one's sales by three percent or more we're way ahead."

"But they could be learning all that from their manager while they travel together in the territory. At the same time, they'd be meeting the customers and learning about their problems."

"The manager could teach them some of this while they're traveling together. How much sense can they make of what the manager tells them and of what they see on sales calls if they don't have a complete understanding of how things work back at home base? They'd get the story in bits and pieces and wouldn't know near as well what to do to help a customer. But if they work in the plant, they get to know firsthand the people they can turn to, and the things they can do to help."

"The sales reps aren't going to learn that much about a department in the two days they spend in it. I don't know that it's going to make that much of a difference."

"They certainly won't know near as much as the people who work in that department. If you were a new sales rep, would working two days in each department help you understand much better what's happening in your sales calls? The new sales rep could relate the customers' needs to how the company would handle them. When they're traveling with the manager, they'll learn everything much more thoroughly, and much faster."

"But we're doing okay now. So why spend the extra money?"

"We're making sales and profits, too. What do you think of trying it on a couple of sales reps? Doing okay doesn't seem as good if we could be doing still better."

"All right, we'll give it a try. Maybe we ought to ask the experienced sales reps how much they think it would've helped them."

"Great idea. I'll get started on it right away."

Reducing Your Own Resistance

Using this method of responding to objections keeps your own resistance down as well as lowering the other person's. It's hard for you to resist an idea unreasonably if you first have to acknowledge something in it that you agree with.

Furthermore, asking a question about the idea rather than arguing back makes you open-minded about it. And in telling why you're asking, you're sharing your reasoning with the other person. With your question, you're inviting him to tell his reasoning so that the both of you can look at both reasonings and decide together on the weight of the evidence.

Taking this reasonable approach means that you can profit from good ideas presented to you. This method also builds your credibility since it shows that you're going by the facts.

‖9‖ Constructive Persuading

Handling Objections by Creating Solutions

You can deal effectively with an objection either by bringing out its error, or by bringing up a constructive approach to it. In both methods, you first acknowledge what's true or worth considering in the objection, and then inquire into either his error or your constructive way.

Suppose a district sales manager is trying to persuade his boss, the general sales manager, to drop the new requirement that all salespersons to be hired must have prior experience in selling the same kinds of products that this company sells. The district manager would then have many more salespersons to choose from. He feels that it's much easier to teach the needed product knowledge than to find applicants with high sales ability and drive.

The general sales manager replies:

"They've got to have experience with our products. Remember how that last salesperson you hired messed up his sales calls? He never learned the products. He couldn't talk intelligently about them."

"You're right, he didn't know our products well enough. Why do you think that because one salesperson doesn't learn our products, others won't? It might be that he was lazy about studying the products. Others might apply themselves to it."

The district manager is focusing his question on the general sales manager's reasoning error that because this salesperson didn't learn, all salespersons who, like him, have no experience with these products also won't learn. The general sales manager would be hard pressed to support her objection once she's faced with her flawed reasoning. She's likely to move to another objection; or if she's defensive, insist she's right without supporting it; or if she's reasonable, concede your point and ask what you think the requirements should be.

This is one good way of handling the objection. It's likely to succeed unless the general sales manager feels threatened by having her reasoning error exposed, and reacts by trying to justify her objection with further reasoning errors. If you have an open, easy relationship with the other person and he's reasonable, you can use this successfully.

Another way that the district manager could have responded is through a constructive inquiry as follows:

"You're right, he didn't work out. Why don't we require that all new salespeople have successful sales experience in industrial sales? If they mastered product knowledge in previous jobs, they're likely to master ours."

This constructive approach has the big advantage of reducing defensiveness by not confronting the other person with his reasoning error. While it requires you to see the reasoning error, you don't have to point to it. This makes it easier emotionally, but you have to create a way of working on or solving the problem. Being constructive can also be stimulating and challenging. Both ways enhance your image. Inquiring into reasoning to bring out the error marks you as keenly analytical, while the constructive approach presents you as creative.

The Advantage of the Constructive Inquiry

We tend to reach for a constructive solution only when the objection is logical and realistic. We have no other alternative. If we don't find a way around the objection, it will stop our idea. But when the objection is false, our impulse is to bring out its error and confront the other person with it. We feel that logic is on our side so we'll triumph. The trouble is, we often come up against a stubborn defensiveness that resists logic.

But even with a false objection we can often use the constructive approach. While the other person knows within him that his objection is false, he might not want to admit he made a reasoning error. If we suggest a solution that skirts the objection's error instead of spotlighting it, the other person is much more likely to respond favorably. The focus is shifted to the solution, the objection fades away unnoticed, and the other person saves face.

Another advantage in using the constructive inquiry is that emotionally it's much easier to ask the question. It can be difficult to ask the other person about his reasoning when it may very well contain an error, and your asking could make him defensive.

It's much more comfortable to inquire about whether a suggestion you have in mind is acceptable. This isn't threatening to the other person. You're not confronting him with any holes in his reasoning.

To illustrate, if the other person bases his objection on generalizing from a single case, your reply feels much less adversarial if you say, "Wouldn't it be worthwhile to look at a few more cases to make sure?" than it does if you ask, "Can we really come to that conclusion from just one case?"

There are times when the other person hasn't revealed enough about his objection for you to respond either constructively or by focusing on his reasoning. You have to inquire into his objection; and often when you do, a reasoning error pops out. Your first impulse might be to point out this reasoning error. Control the impulse. Use the constructive inquiry as the first choice, with the inquiry that aims at bringing out a reasoning error as a fallback alternative.

Suppose a sales manager wants to persuade a salesperson to stop overvisiting her friendly accounts. The salesperson is making 80 percent of her calls on the companies that are giving her 80 percent of her business, leaving only 20 percent of her calls for getting new business from prospects who are giving her little or none. The sales manager has just told the salesperson that she might increase sales by as much as 50 percent if she would switch 30 percent of her calls from her good customers to prospects and customers who give her very little of their business. Let's watch the manager use the constructive inquiry in the rest of the conversation, starting with the salesperson's reply:

"I can't do that. I'd lose business from my good customers. They know from my being there so much that I really care about them and want to give them good service. They're used to it."

"I'm sure they're happy with you and with our products or they wouldn't give you so much business. What would you think of cutting down on your calls to them very gradually, say five percent a month, so that they'd not even notice it? They'd get used to it. That way in six months you'd be spending fifty percent of your calls building new business and moving toward increasing your sales and income by fifty percent."

"It wouldn't work out that way. I'd come out behind. There's very little business to be had from these other companies. That's why I make so few calls on them. It's a waste. I'm putting the calls where they pay off, and I don't want to lose the good customers."

"You've certainly got a good chunk of the business in your territory. How about your talking with the market research people? They've got a good picture of your territory—how large the market is and the potential in each company. You'd pick up valuable information for getting more buisness."

"I know my territory. I'm out there much more than they are, and I'm working it in the most productive way."

"Yes, you're out there a lot more. Isn't it possible that you'd gain something by looking at their information, since they use different methods for evaluationg a territory's potential? And you'd have nothing to lose by doing it."

"Okay, I'll take a look. Maybe I'll learn something. But I can't cut down my calls on my good customers. That's where my business is. I can't afford to lose any."

"You certainly don't want to lose any. If you were the customer, how would you feel about a salesperson who visits you every other week? You place orders with him only once a month, and can even do so by phone."

"I see what you mean. I'd think the salesperson is running scared, and using up my time. It's tough out there. I guess I am running a little scared. Listen, I'll get with market research, and then I'll see about working out a new plan where I switch some calls a little at a time."

If the sales manager were to handle each objection by trying to bring out the reasoning error in it, he could respond to the first objection by saying: "It's important to give good service. Why do you think you would lose their business if you cut down on calls to them? You could give them the good service they need with fewer calls, especially since they can always reach you by phone."

To the second objection he might reply: "You're right to put the calls where they pay off. What makes you think that there's little business to be had from the other companies? According to market research, there's a big potential there."

To the third objection his response could be: "Yes, you are in the territory much more than market research is. Do you really think their findings aren't worth considering compared to yours? They're professionals and they use methods designed specifically to evaluate the market potential."

For the fourth objection, the sales manager used a role reversal. He asked the salesperson to put herself in the place of the customer. This technique is a very effective third kind of method that is really closer to getting the other person to see his reasoning error. He sees it much more readily when he looks at it from the vantage point of someone else.

The constructive inquiry feels less confrontational than does the inquiry into the other person's reasoning. You're asking him for his reaction to a way you're suggesting solving the problem, rather than asking him to defend his objection.

How to Know What Question to Ask

The objections you encounter in trying to persuade are either reasonable ones, or those that arise from resistance. Remember, you'll almost always encounter some resistance. It might come from the other person's need to put off a decision until he has assimilated your idea and gotten used to it. Often, there are other causes of resistance (competitiveness, fear of change) as well.

The reasonable objection is easy to handle. It's only a question of examining the facts on both sides and going by the weight of the evidence. If the objection is one that you hadn't taken into account, you have to either find some way to handle it, or weigh it against the benefits to see if your idea is worth using.

However, most of the objections by far arise from resistance.

This kind is very likely to contain a reasoning error; for the objection is then probably a rationalization contrived to make the resistance appear reasonable. Such objections are more difficult to deal with and require the use of either a constructive inquiry, or one that brings out the reasoning error.

When a person raises an objection, he is predicting that a particular problem will arise. The reasoning error lies in the basis of this prediction. How does he know the problem will arise? His error is that he can't know that it will, based on the evidence he points to.

The following five reasoning errors are the ones that you're likely to encounter most frequently in objections to your ideas:

1. GENERALIZING FROM A SINGLE CASE. "There's no point in taking out a service contract on that new machine for the first year even though the warranty is for only three months. It's a waste of money. I bought the same model a year ago and it hasn't needed a single repair."

2. FALSE ANALOGY (seeing things that are alike in some way as being the same in all respects). "I find that engineers don't write clearly and to the point. Did you ever see Doris's writing? It's hard to figure out what she's getting at. She must have an engineering background."

3. ALL OR NONE. "You won't get anywhere counseling Tom on his being more cooperative with the people he works with. You can't change people." (You can change some things in some people, to varying degrees. This is also called an either-or error. Things are thought of as being either one way or another, rather than ever being in between.)

4. UNSUPPORTED ASSERTIONS. "Most people don't want to take responsibility. That's why I have to supervise so closely." (This

is an assertion that is very likely not based on any evidence but is just an assumption.)

5. AFTER IT, THEREFORE CAUSED BY IT (if a particular thing generally happens after another specific thing occurs, the first must be caused by the second). "There doesn't seem to be much interest in that new service we're offering. The ad I wrote up didn't pull as well as I hoped it would." (The lack of response might have been caused by the ad rather than by low interest in the service.)

The first thing to do when you encounter an objection is to see if one of these five reasoning errors is present. As you become more familiar with them, you'll spot the reasoning error more quickly. Soon you'll see it almost instantly. If you don't, you can pause for a moment before answering; or if you need more time, say to the other person: "That's an interesting point. Let me think about it for a moment." He'll be flattered by your giving it so much thought.

When you find the reasoning error, form your reply using a constructive inquiry as the first choice. But use an inquiry into reasoning if it seems more appropriate, or if a constructive one doesn't occur to you.

To form the constructive inquiry, ask to either look for more information to find out whether the objection is really so; or ask if a suggestion you have can be tried. To form the reasoning inquiry, ask whether one could really predict what will happen based on the reasoning error. However, don't refer to it as an error. Keep in mind that you start both inquiry remarks with an acknowledgment of something true or worth considering in his objection. This disarms both you and him to prevent the adversary stance.

Let's apply the forming of both constructive and reasoning inquiry remarks to each of the five objections used above:

1. GENERALIZING FROM A SINGLE CASE. "There's no point in taking out a service contract on that new machine for the first year even though the warranty is for only three months. I bought the same model a year ago and it hasn't needed a single repair."

Constructive Inquiry: "Your experience does suggest putting off a service contract. Why don't we check on the first-year record of a few more of these machines just to make sure?"

Reasoning Inquiry: "Your experience does suggest putting off a service contract. Do you think that we should base our decision on just one machine's performance? Maybe this machine is unusually sturdy, just as another one might be a lemon. Or maybe your use of it was different.

2. FALSE ANALOGY (seeing things that are alike in some ways as being the same in all respects). "I find that engineers don't write clearly and to the point. Did you ever see Doris's writing? It's hard to understand what she's getting at. She must have an engineering background."

Constructive Inquiry: "It's true her writing isn't clear. Why don't we find out about her background? It might help us make fuller use of her skills."

Reasoning Inquiry: "It's true, her writing isn't clear. Don't you get letters and memos and reports from a lot of people who don't write clearly and who aren't engineers? Maybe Doris is one of those."

3. ALL-OR-NONE (EITHER-OR). "You won't get anywhere counseling Tom on being more cooperative with the people he works with. You can't change people."

Constructive inquiry: "There are people you can't do anything with. Still, couldn't we give it a try? Tom just might be more responsive than most."

Reasoning inquiry: "There are people you can't do anything with. Aren't there also people you can change in some ways, at least to some extent? If I could just make a little progress with Tom about this one thing, it would be a big help."

4. UNSUPPORTED ASSERTION. "Most people don't want to take responsibility. That's why I have to supervise so closely."

Constructive inquiry: "Some people are like that. Why don't you take your two most reliable people and try letting them work on their own a little more? If it works out, you could try it with some others. Maybe they just need more of a chance."

Reasoning inquiry: "Some people are like that. Is it possible that your people are not taking responsibility because you're supervising them so closely, rather than the other way around?"

5. OCCURRING AFTER IT, THEREFORE CAUSED BY IT. "There doesn't seem to be much interest in that new service we're offering. The ad I wrote up and placed didn't pull as well as I hoped it would."

Constructive inquiry: "The low response could indicate that. How about writing up a different ad? Maybe it's not the service but the way you're advertising it."

Reasoning inquiry: "The low response could indicate that. But couldn't it mean instead that the ad isn't doing the job right, either, because of the way it's written or the publication it's placed in?"

Finding the Reasoning Errors

Let's look at the reasoning errors in the following conversation:

"We need someone with an accounting background in this sales job. John has been an accountant for the past eight years. I think he'd be right for this position." (False analogy: John shares one characteristic with people who succeed in this job. Therefore, he's like them in all other characteristics as well.)

"But John has never done any selling. We don't know if he would be any good at it."

"Selling is just a matter of being good with people and communicating your ideas well. [Unsupported assertion.] John gets along very well with everyone and he certainly communicates clearly."

"But we don't even know if he wants to sell. He might not like it at all."

"Relax. All you need to do is motivate him. Look at Nancy. She didn't want to go into selling. But I gave her a good increase in salary and told her what it could mean for her career and now she's out there loving it." [Generalizing from a single case.]

"If we put him in the job, it could take a year to find out whether he's suitable for it. If he's not, it's going to cost us a lot of money. It seems pretty risky to me, considering his lack of sales experience."

"You've got to take risks in business if you want to succeed. Any decision involves risks." [Either-or error: This reply implies that either you take risks or you don't, that it's all or none rather than your being able to take various amounts of risk.]

"It seems to me we'd do better if we hired someone with successful sales experience who has some knowledge of accounting. After all, you don't have to be an accountant for this sales job. You just need the kind of basic understanding that lots of businesspeople have. And we could add to this fairly quickly. What we need is a good salesperson."

"I wish that were true, but in almost all cases when I've hired from the outside for this job, the person didn't succeed." [Occurring after it, therefore caused by it: He wrongly concludes that the person didn't succeed because he was hired from the outside. Actually, the hiring failures might have occurred because of poor methods of recruiting or selecting.]

Applying the Constructive Inquiry

The constructive inquiry has the great advantage of keeping down the other person's defensiveness when you're dislodging his objection. And it's more pleasant for him to discuss what can be done about something than it is to talk about what's wrong with his reasoning.

Let's see how you would form the constructive inquiry for objections that contain the five most common reasoning errors:

1. GENERALIZING FROM A SINGLE CASE

"That agency Fran recommended so highly isn't good. I tried them last week. I needed a typist for the day and the person they sent was very slow."

"That would discourage you. How about checking with some of their other customers? You could ask the agency for their names. Maybe their one time was an error that slipped through."

2. FALSE ANALOGY

Ask whether the generality applies in this particular case.

"Let me tell you why Joe is asking for a raise. If you compliment an employee a few times for good work, he'll ask for more money. You must have been giving him a lot of compliments."

"I have complimented Joe when he's done good work. Could we take a close look at his performance to see if he deserves a raise? He hasn't had one in two years because of our freeze, and I'd hate to lose him."

3. ALL-OR-NONE (EITHER-OR)

Ask about finding out if some are different.

"I don't want to use plastic. It breaks too easily. I'd rather play it safe with metal."

"Some plastics do break more easily than we could tolerate.

Why don't we try testing a stronger plastic in this particular situation. If the plastic works, we'd save a lot of money."

4. Unsupported Assertion

Ask about trying something that either tests or counters the assertion. "If we let the supervisors have the regularly scheduled meetings they want, they'll use having to attend the meetings as an excuse when they fall behind in their work."

"We don't want to give them a reason for falling behind. What if we have them vote on whether to have these meetings? That way they'd be taking responsibility for fitting in the meetings and still keeping up. Actually, the meetings might save time in the long run."

5. Occurring After It, Therefore Caused by It

Ask about looking for other possible causes.

"In the three months that Jean has been supervisor of that unit, two of her people have left. I told you she wouldn't make a good supervisor."

"If that rate of turnover continues, it's much too high. Shouldn't we find out why they left? Maybe it had nothing to do with Jean."

Since using the constructive inquiry helps prevent the adversary stance, it contributes greatly to your effectiveness in persuading. It's hard to argue against either getting more information about the objection, or doing something about it. Your reasonableness encourages the other person to be reasonable; and he's likely to feel good about your taking his objection seriously enough to do something about it.

At first, it may seem difficult to analyze for reasoning errors quickly enough. But keep in mind that an objection is just a prediction that some specific thing will happen to make your idea unworkable. All you need do is ask yourself, can the other person reasonably expect that specific thing to happen based on the reason he gives?

Reasoning errors are not that complicated. Detecting them doesn't require a deep, extensive study of logic. The rules of reasoning arise from everyday experience. And you use them every day. You can also readily find the reasoning errors. Put them in mind during a discussion and listen closely, rather than thinking of the arguments you're going to give back.

Let's listen to the selling of an idea using the constructive approach:

"We ought to set up a program of short courses that the employees could take when they get off from work. They'd do a better job if they took courses that improved their performance, and it wouldn't require time off the job. And if they took courses related to their personal interests, such as personal finance or cooking, it would improve morale since they'd gain knowledge and skill in things they're interested in at no cost to them."

"People aren't going to want to hang around taking courses after a full day's work. They're going to want to get home and relax."

"Many of them would feel like going home. What if we take a survey to see how many would sign up for courses? Other companies are doing this successfully."

"If we asked them to come on their own time, we'd have to provide a lot of courses that they're interested in that wouldn't improve their job performance. Only a few are likely to take job-related courses. We'd be spending a lot of money for nothing."

"If it turned out that way, it's true, we'd gain mainly in improved morale. Suppose we draw up a list of possible courses, including both job-related and those having to do with personal interests? We could then ask the employees which they would sign up for if offered."

"They might say they'd take certain courses and then not

show up for them. Meanwhile, we'd have contracted for instructors and arranged for space."

"This could happen. What if we try it on a small scale. Just contract for a few courses first, say the two job-related ones and the two that are only interest-related that have the largest enrollment. We would tell the employees that our extending and continuing the program would depend on their attendance. That way we'd risk very little."

"People won't come to job-related courses on their own time. They'd expect us to give them the time to go."

"Many would. But why couldn't we wait to go ahead with anything until they enroll? A lot of courses such as oral communication skills, more effective writing, problem solving, time management, and how to use a computer overlap both personal interests and job activities for many people."

"All right. Draw up a list of courses and we'll see what they want, if anything."

To use the constructive inquiry most effectively, try to anticipate the objections that might arise. This gives you more time to think of constructive suggestions for dealing with the objections. Since you then have only the unexpected objections to contend with on the spot, you're much more likely to sell your idea. And you'll come across as someone whose mind works quickly and productively.

‖10‖ Dealing with Others' Feelings

The Power of Gut Feelings

"Why do you still feel it won't work? We've worked out all the objections you raised. And look at the benefits. Besides, it's worked in other places."

"I've got this feeling that there's something wrong with it. I've worked here long enough so I can usually tell whether something is right."

"With all your experience, we should look into your feeling. What do you feel is wrong with it? Maybe we could change the idea so it would feel right."

"I can't put my finger on it. It comes from my gut. And I don't like to go against my gut feeling. I remember being sorry when I did."

Whether we call it a gut feeling, an intuition, or a hunch, we develop it by unconsciously combining the available evidence, past experience, and perhaps some wishful thinking to make up an immediate total feeling. We're not aware of the parts that contribute to this feeling. We just feel it as a whole.

Since we didn't arrive at our intuition through logical analysis, we don't know if it's valid. How much of the intuition is based on evidence, and is the evidence valid? Is the past-experience portion relevant? To what extent does wishful thinking affect the intuition? The intuition could be right or wrong depending on its makeup. Using it means taking a calculated risk.

Whether you're faced with the other person's intuition or your own, here are some points to guide you:

1. If the intuition is strong, and it contradicts the evidence, try to work out where it comes from, and also reevaluate the evidence.

2. If you don't have enough evidence to make a logical decision, and you have to act now, use intuition. It's the only thing you have.

3. In selling an idea, don't use your intuition as though it were evidence. Unless you have a marvelous demonstrated track record of success with it, your intuition isn't convincing. After all, how much would the other person's intuition convince you? A good track record is well above fifty percent right. You get fifty percent by just tossing a coin.

We React Emotionally and Out of Habit, Not Reasoning

When we encounter any situation, we react on two levels simultaneously: a reasoning level and a feeling level. These are separate reactions, independent of each other. You can feel fear when your reasoning tells you there's nothing to be afraid of. That's why your own gut feeling can oppose your reasoned conclusion.

It's a curious thing that many people readily acknowledge

that feelings aren't logical, that you don't reason to the feeling you're supposed to have, and then have it. Yet, these same people act as though they believe the opposite by saying: "There's no reason for you to be angry at that. It just turned out that way accidentally. Nobody meant to inconvenience you."

Suppose someone borrows your stepladder and doesn't return it. As a result, you don't have it when you want it. You become angry at him. You reasoned that he deprived you of the stepladder's use. And you learned the habit of becoming angry when someone deprives you. Anyone reasoning from the same facts would have to agree that he deprived you. But everyone wouldn't get angry if it happened to him. It depends on what he learned emotionally.

Some people might make a distinction between whether the borrower deprived them uncaringly or accidentally. Did he not return the stepladder because he decided to watch a TV program instead and figured you could wait a little longer? Or did he truly forget because of something that suddenly came up that he had to attend to? They'd learned to get angry at the first but not at the second.

While they reason to what happened, they learned to react angrily to an uncaring act but not to an accidental one. Others might get angry either way, because they learned to react that way whenever they're deprived.

One person who made a decision that turned out wrong might be embarrassed by it. Another person who did the same thing in the same circumstances might just feel he can't win them all. He didn't have enough information but he had to make a decision.

A gut feeling is a clue worth considering. But you can't tell how much significance it has unless you track down where it comes from. The problem is, the person who has the gut feeling generally overestimates the chances that it's right.

When the other person has a negative gut feeling about

your idea, he generally won't be able to tell right off why he has this feeling. We don't analyze or reason with our feelings. We just react. Still, the feeling presses him. If he's anxious that your idea will get him into trouble, he'll resist even though he doesn't know the source of the feeling.

The Reasoning Errors in Gut Feelings

Gut feelings can readily contain some wrong reasoning. If they turn out right, it's usually because the person who made them used the gut feelings in combination with reasoning. Often, much of a particular gut feeling about a present idea occurs because the idea is similar to the past idea that originally evoked that feeling.

If a present idea is somewhat similar to a past idea, the present idea evokes in us the same feeling that the past idea did when it was applied. Whatever differences there are between the two ideas reduce just the intensity of the feeling. But on a thinking level, if we know what these differences are, we might readily see that they are critical, and our later idea is likely to turn out very differently from the result of the earlier one. This is why our gut feeling often contains a false analogy. We react as though any resemblance we find between the present and past ideas means that they're completely alike. Our feelings don't notice the differences.

We also generalize from a single instance. For this feeling from the past arises whenever we encounter similar ideas to the past one. It's as though all ideas similar in some way to the original one deserve this gut feeling. And we'll do all-or-none thinking since the gut feeling is either positive or negative, and occurs to all similar ideas. So if something like our idea didn't work in the past, the gut feeling is that it won't work now, rather than that it'll work to a certain extent or for certain situations.

Be wary of deciding by gut feelings alone. But don't ignore them, particularly if you have a strong one. Try hard to figure out where it comes from, and evaluate carefully any evidence that contradicts it.

The Fear of Risk

Life is full of risk. Some people are more comfortable with risk than others.

Buying any idea imposes risk, and a buyer who fears risk will continually look for assurances. He'll scrutinize every possible threat. Since he might be self-conscious about his anxious fingering of every angle, it's helpful to be patient and supportive. Otherwise, he might end the discussion so that he doesn't risk your thinking he's a worrier.

Risk is particularly threatening to those who are embarrassed by losing. A number of people feel ashamed of having any misfortune. For the moment, whether the loss is beyond their control or arises from their doing, they feel marked as losers. They don't want to risk having this feeling.

Another emotional loss on top of the actual loss is the feeling of incompetence that comes from making a wrong decision. Even when they make the best decision possible, based on the information available, if it turns out badly, they feel that somehow they could have done better.

When the other person mentions some risk, ask him to tell you more about it as a way of getting him to air his feelings. His feelings have less force when they're brought out than when they're buried inside him. You'll probably have to encourage him to talk because people resist talking about their feelings. They're never quite sure that in talking about the feelings they're willing to reveal, they'll be able to keep out the ones they don't want to face or admit to.

Let's listen to the latter part of an idea-selling conversation:

"Your idea sounds good. I'm just afraid the people who have to carry it out are going to mess it up."

"We have to make sure they can handle it. Do you think the things they'd have to do are any more difficult than what they're now doing?"

"No, I guess not. They're doing okay with things just as complicated. It's just that whenever you make a change, there's room for trouble."

"It could happen. How did it go the last time you made a change?"

"Very well. We went over everything very carefully with them beforehand and even did a few dry runs. That way they worked out problems before they could happen. They got the feel of it."

"Well, if you worked it out with them that way again, don't you think these changes should be handled just as well?"

"Probably, but you never know for sure."

"That's true. But even though you never know for sure, haven't you made things turn out real well with your decisions?"

"Yes, I have. Okay, let's go with it."

How the Facts Can Make You Angry

When someone strongly resists an idea, the piling up of the favorable facts can anger him. They cause an inner conflict between resisting and being reasonable. Conflict is frustrating, and frustration causes anger.

We depend so much on logic to convince people that when they respond with anger to our reasonable approach, we become helpless. Generally, if we persist at all, we resort to repeating the same logical arguments. We figure that the other person didn't absorb our logic.

We forget that although we say we always want to do the

logical thing because we're reasonable, we respond more strongly to our motivations, right or wrong. We use logic as a tool for getting what we want, whether it helps or hurts us. We bend logic when we want something that's unreasonable, and straighten it when being reasonable gets us to our goal.

While people generally know this, they usually don't deal with it. Perhaps they don't fully accept it. After all, in school we learn how to think and express ourselves reasonably. We don't learn anything about coping with unreasonableness even though we encounter so much of it.

When the other person becomes angry as you develop more support for your idea, you might as well pull back. Rather than trying to overwhelm his resistance by piling up evidence, it might be better to focus on reducing his resistance. A good way to do this is to bring it into the open.

Listen to this husband trying to sell an idea to his wife.

"Ellen wants me to do some consulting for her company. It's a good chance for me to get a start in consulting. I can do it evenings and weekends."

"I don't think it's a good idea. Concentrate on your regular job. You'll be better off."

"Why? I like consulting and I want to go out on my own. Maybe this will lead to other things."

"Consulting's too risky. You've got a good job. You can get ahead in it."

"Don't you think you can get laid off in any job? Look at Larry, after twelve years. Besides, I'm not going to take any chances. I'll hold my job until I have enough consulting work to make a living. Who knows, I might make a lot more money. And if it didn't work out, I could get another job."

"You and your smart ideas. You can't see when you're well off. You make me sick. A lot of people would love to have your job. It's interesting, varied, you make good money, and here you're thinking of throwing it away. Why don't you grow up? You've got a wife and two children to support."

The husband could make the mistake here of showing all the reasons why consulting was worth trying. This would only make his wife angrier. Instead, he tries to get at the basis of her resistance.

"There must be something else bothering you or you wouldn't be so angry. Can we talk about it?"

"Who's angry? I'm just giving my opinion. There's one thing I'm wondering about. How much time is this consulting for Ellen going to take?"

"Maybe about six hours a week for about four months. I could do a couple of hours in the evening and the rest on Saturday. Why?"

"Just wondering. And if you get another consulting job at the same time, when would you handle that? In the evening and on Sunday? And if you did, when would you have time for your family?"

"You're right. For the time being, it could cut into my family life. But if I could get two more consulting jobs, I'd have three going at the same time. Then I'd quit my job and try to get more. If I did that, we'd have a lot more time together. We could work together if you'd like. You'd handle the office and working up of promotional literature. Who knows, together we might make it into the big time. But I'd like to give it a year, anyway, and then we'd take another look. Do you think you could take the hard part for a year?"

"I don't know. You make it sound good. Let's talk about it some more."

Responding to Emotional Pressure

The other person's emotional pressure that's unrelated to your idea may be affecting his reactions. Something else that's making him anxious may have used up his emotional capacity to bear risk: a criticism from his boss, or a failure in some project, might have depressed him and made him unresponsive; he might be distracted by anger from some current frustration.

People express their emotions in different ways. While some get excited, others conceal their agitation and let their feelings seep out in quiet ways such as sarcasm, indifference, and inattention.

Since feelings can retard the absorbing of information, increase jumping to wrong conclusions, and interfere with reasoning, it's helpful to remain sensitive to emotional reactions. Often, you can drain off the other person's feelings by getting him to talk; or you can lead him to control them by getting him to focus on them. When the feelings are too intense, it might be better to put off the conversation.

We have to be alert to feelings, for they might intrude at any moment on the conversation. Often, we're so intent on the logic that we overlook the feeling unless it's a screaming one. When you hear a feeling, respond to it. Point to it to show the other person that you caught it, and to get him to think about it. If it's clear what's causing the feeling, acknowledge that it's an understandable reaction that anyone might have. This makes the other person feel comfortable talking about it. Ask about the feeling. This helps him let out the pressure so that he can think more sensibly.

Watch the responding to feelings in this conversation:

"I think this ad is just what we need to give us a little more of the leading edge, new horizons. Why don't you show this to the boss and tell him how important it is that we start building our image in this direction. Tell him we all feel that way."

"I'd like to, but you know how the boss sticks to the wave of the past. He likes to tell them where we came from, not where we're going. I'm afraid he'd stomp all over me."

"I can understand your being anxious. He can get wild if

you mess with his viewpoints. Is there any way you could just wave it in front of him while talking about something else, just to plant the beginnings of the idea?"

"It's pretty risky. The last time I tried that he gave me a chilly stare that made me shiver in July; and he growled at me that either I get to the point or I get out."

"He can be rough. If it's okay with you, I'll show it to him, and talk gently about it."

"Look, the boss could be right. We've come a long way in the past ten years with this traditional image. How much the hell do you know about this business, anyway? Guys like you, after a couple of years you think you know it all."

"You're right, I have a lot less experience and maybe I'm seeing it wrong. What happened that made you angry? If it's something I said, maybe I could learn not to do it again."

"It got to me, your playing the hero and making me look weak."

"I get that way, too, when someone pushes me to do something I feel I should but don't want to."

"I didn't say I feel I should."

"No, you didn't, but do you? Because you called me a hero for being willing to."

"Well, I guess so. But you've got to do this in small steps."

"Right. What do you say we work out something for an image that's not in the future and not in the past but in that place in between. What do you call it again?"

"The present. Okay, work something up and we'll take a look."

Each Person Has His Own Emotional Norm

When someone erupts much more loudly than we would if we were angry, we tend to think that he's much angrier than he is. We forget that people vary in how expressive they are.

Some explode at a small irritation while others suppress every-thing that's less than a seething rage. Some easily bare their worry, envy, impatience, and joy while others conceal all but the strongest feelings.

To understand another's feeling we have to judge it by how far it is above his emotional norm. For someone who trips off easily, a sudden outburst of anger may pass quickly as a sum-mer breeze. A growl from someone who seldom growls may mean far more anger than a roar from someone who always roars.

While we can understand the concept that people vary in how emotionally expressive they are, it's difficult for us to feel this and therefore believe it since we've never been anyone but ourselves.

When we're calm, we can more easily go by what we in-tellectually know. But in moments of stress, we often fall back on old habits or gut feelings. Facing someone's emotions gen-erally stresses us, and our own feelings come into play. Since under stress it's difficult to contemplate what we intellectually know, we turn to our own reactions with the feeling that hers are the same. Often, we read her feelings wrongly.

Listen to this conversation:

"Did you see my reading glasses? I can't find them any-where. There's some stuff I've got to read. Please help me find them. I can't do anything without them."

"Why don't you have a particular place to keep each thing? You waste a lot of time looking for glasses and other things you keep losing."

(Angrily.) "Stop preaching at me. I've got a lot on my mind. I can't keep track of everything. So I'm not organized. Help me. Don't just sit there telling me what's wrong with me. I could tell you a few things about yourself. Dammit, I'm sick of your criticism."

"I'm just trying to save you from wasting time. But if you

don't appreciate it, the hell with it. You're so goddamn defensive, nobody can tell you anything."

"Look who's talking. A little criticism and you go to pieces. [Finds glasses.] Oh, here they are. I don't know how I missed them. I'm sure I looked there. Say, there's a good movie at the Plaza and the timing is right."

"Who the hell wants to go to a movie? I'm so goddamn mad, I can't even talk to you."

"What made you so angry suddenly?

"Your anger made me angry, that's what."

"Who's angry? I'm not angry."

"Didn't you just blow up when I made a sensible suggestion about your glasses?"

"That was before. I let it all out and now it's gone."

"But now I'm angry and I can't let go of it. It's sticking."

"You should let it all out. You'll feel better."

"I wish I could. I don't know how, but I'll try. We'll have a lot more noise around here."

"But it won't last long."

If you think about the emotional reactions of the people you know well, you'll see that each individual has his own characteristic duration of an emotional reaction. Unless you know a person well, you won't know the significance of his emotional reaction. When you're selling an idea, don't withdraw too quickly in the face of anger. Stay with it a little longer. It may blow over quickly. And watch that you don't attribute the same meaning to the other person's reaction as you would to your own if you were to react that way.

Your Feelings Arouse Feelings in the Other Person

Most emotions feel uncomfortable. Joy is an exception. This discomfort is nature's way of helping us survive. Fear, anger, guilt, suspicion, envy, shame, all motivate us to do something in order to get rid of the discomfort. When an uncomfortable feeling intrudes into your discussion, it's likely to hinder the selling of your idea.

When you become frustrated by the other person's resistance, your irritation might get away from you in little ways that you don't notice but that register on the other person. Your eyebrows might rise, your eyes widen, your voice get a little louder. Your humor might have a little bite in it, or may turn into sarcasm. Your head might shake or your fists clench.

When the other person senses your anger, it's likely to evoke in him anger or fear. This distracts him from thinking about your idea and makes him uncomfortable. To get rid of the discomfort, it's much easier for him to end the discussion than to buy your idea.

If you're anxious in the discussion, you're likely to communicate it unwittingly. You talk too fast and too much. You're apologetic and too eager to please. You repeat yourself. You give up too easily or push too hard.

The other person sees all this and wonders why you're worried. Are you unsure of the worth of your idea? Do you feel incompetent to sell it? She becomes reluctant to move on your idea.

When you see emotional reactions in the other person, look inwardly at your feelings. You might be communicating what you're feeling, which is causing the other person's reactions. If you feel you might be, try to relax. Settle back in your chair. Calm yourself by smiling and taking a few deep breaths.

Encouraging Expression of Feelings

As soon as you see emotion in the other person, try to get him to talk, preferably about his feelings. Stop presenting, and explore his reasoning. You might say that he seems irritated or worried about something, and you're wondering what it is. Perhaps there has been a misunderstanding or you can help in some way.

Then let him talk. Don't refute something you disagree with, or tell him he's wrong, or explain something to him. Ask him questions to get him to continue until he seems calmed down. Don't discuss his logic at this point.

What you have in your favor is that he probably wants to talk. He wants to discharge his feelings in order to get more comfortable. Help him. Don't in any way criticize his feelings. Support him by telling him how his having these feelings is perfectly understandable in the circumstances.

If a person seems angry during your discussion with her and you don't know why, you might be quick to feel that you're causing it. You wonder what you did to make her angry. Since your self-blame hampers your thinking and relating, it's useful at that point to stop selling the idea for the moment and mention that she seems irritated. You'll often find that it has nothing to do with you. This not only relaxes you but is likely to relieve her, as well, as she talks about it.

‖ 11 ‖ Coping with Your Own Feelings

Our Feelings Often Hamper Our Persuading

How do you mentally link up with the other person when you're being bounced around by your own feelings? It isn't easy to maneuver the other person's thinking while wrestling with your emotions. So you need to relax, calm down, keep reminding yourself that if you take it easy, you'll wind up being far more persuasive.

The persuasive interaction triggers off feelings of self-doubt, self-blame, sensitivity to insult, fear of rejection, anger at being frustrated, anxiety about looking incompetent, and guilt about hurting someone. Selling an idea and encountering resistance is bound to bring with it some of these feelings, which arise when there's conflict.

Most of us remember occasions when an apt thing to say crossed our minds but never left our mouths. Or we thought of it when we got out the door. Some feeling inhibited us. Perhaps we doubted our thinking and didn't want to be caught in a mistake. Or we were afraid of offending. It's as though the feeling reaches out and claps a hand over our mouth.

Fear of the Other Person's No

When you're about to sell an idea, it's natural to expect resistance. Otherwise, why would you need to sell? You might also be afraid that at the mention of your idea, the other person will say no without having heard your story. And once he says no, he'll stop listening to your arguments for the idea, and you will have lost the sale.

You now feel the need to get your whole story in before he gets a chance to say no. This leaves you in the self-defeating position of trying to tell all your arguments in your opening remark. But doing this leads to the very thing you were afraid of: He stops listening because he can't absorb it all.

But if he says no, does it have to mean that he'll stop listening? Suppose you get him to explain his no instead of your arguing against it. Why does he say no in view of the benefits? You're providing a basis for discussion and getting him to examine his resistance. You're likely to lose your fear of no if you expect resistance as a natural reaction rather than trying to prevent it; and if you make it a practice to look into it with the other person to see where it comes from.

The Fear of Offending by Questioning

Many people are afraid to ask questions. They view a question as an intrusion, particularly a question that asks the other person to explain her reasoning. This might uncover an error in her thinking and cause her to lose face. If this happened, the person asking the question might feel guilty about inflicting this, or anxious about angering the other person.

People often feel anxious about confronting with a question. They're afraid that the other person will feel as though he's being tested. How does he know that what he says is so? How can it be so when the facts contradict it?

Perhaps it's the very power of questions that makes some people uneasy about using them. Questions push people to face things they don't want to face, to talk about feelings they don't want to reveal, to explain things they don't want to explain. They can wear down and trap people, and suggest motivations that are unsavory.

Yet questions are often necessary to make people reasonable, to reconcile contradictions, and resolve conflicts. To allay your anxiety in asking them, make sure they serve a purpose. And you should tell what that purpose is. Doing this puts the other person at ease for he doesn't have to wonder about what threats the question poses. Putting him at ease makes you more comfortable. It isn't enough to say that you're just curious, or that you'd understand it better. You have to tell what you're wondering about that causes you to ask that question.

Being Anxious About Persisting

Since dealing with resistance is an inevitable part of selling your idea, persisting is essential. But persisting in the face of resistance means being in conflict with the other person. And being in conflict with others makes many people anxious.

The word *conflict* covers all varieties of mutual opposition ranging from disagreement over the meaning of a word all the way to mortal combat. On a feeling level, we don't discriminate as well as we do on a thinking level. Therefore, to varying degrees, the emotional reaction to an argument could be similar to the one to a fist fight. Anger might well up at the other person's resistance to our idea. Emotionally, we're reacting to just being in conflict. On a thinking level, we see the different kinds and degrees of conflict.

If the other person has more power than we do, this intensifies the emotional reaction. The fear of punishment and retaliation tugs at us to stop persisting. As a result, often we don't delve into the disagreement enough to get at its basis.

It's important to glance inwardly at how we feel while we're selling an idea. If we feel anxious, does it seem to come from our persisting in the face of resistance? What are we afraid will happen, and is it likely to? Does it seem reasonable to persist? If so, we have to set aside the anxiety and steel ourselves to continue.

In order to prevent our doing the self-defeating thing, we need to focus on our feelings from time to time. Otherwise, we'll move in directions that are wrong for us without realizing that our feelings are pushing us. We'll have the illusion that we decided intelligently to move that way. If we check on our feelings more often, we'll have fewer regrets that we didn't say a particular thing at the moment it applied.

Anger at the Other Person's Unreasonableness

We get angry when someone resists our idea unreasonably just as we do when someone lies to us. For being unreasonable means denying the truth of the way things are. That seems unfair. We feel that playing by reality is the fundamental rule. We go by however the facts fall.

When the other person invents facts and rationalizes, we feel he's cheating. If the evidence favors using our idea, he should buy it. After all, if circumstances go against our idea, we'll give it up. What often happens is that as the other person becomes unreasonable (doesn't play fair), the anger rises in us and we lose our cool. The other person can then use our emotionality to divert the conversation. Listen to this.

"We need to buy a new machine. This one keeps breaking down. It wastes a lot of time and costs a lot of money to repair."

"We can't afford to buy a new machine as long as this one is still working. We need the money for too many other things. Get it repaired properly."

"I get it repaired properly all the time. We're using the repair service of the company that sold us the machine. We've been using them since we bought it. The trouble is, there are so many worn parts that after we replace one, pretty soon another breaks and the machine stops working."

"Replace all the worn parts. That should solve it."

"It would cost almost as much as buying a new machine. And we wouldn't have the useful features that the new machines have. Besides, there are other parts that will soon become worn. Then we'll have the machine breaking down again."

"Sounds to me like that company is trying to sell you a new machine. It's natural. Everyone's looking for more business. Why don't you try another repair firm, one that doesn't sell new machines?"

"[Voice rises in exasperation.] Because this one has given excellent service. The repair person showed me all the worn parts and exactly how they cause breakdown, and why it would be very economical to buy a new one. In fact, we can't afford the waste in keeping this one. It's already three years older than the average life of the machine."

"Well, we probably got a really superior one, just as someone got a lemon. It's a matter of luck. Ours might last several more years."

"[In an angry tone.] How the hell do you expect me to do this job when the equipment I have keeps breaking down?"

"What are you getting so angry about? I don't think you're

in the mood to discuss this reasonably. Maybe you better cool down and we'll talk about it some more later."

If you expect to get resistance as a natural reaction and have a way of dealing effectively with it, you can relax, wait for it, and respond calmly. After the other person's first response where he says, "We can't afford a new machine," and "Get it repaired properly," you could reply, "I could get it repaired properly again. If I continue doing this, I figure that the amount we'll lose in repair costs and productivity would pay for the new machine in a year. Can we afford not to buy a new machine?"

Wanting to Conquer

As the other person resists, you find yourself wanting to defeat him. For the moment, he is the enemy blocking you. You wield your weapons of words and logic, and thrust them at him. When he continues to resist, you explain again and again as though to dislodge him from his position with repetition.

Your feeling of attacking works against you. Hammering at him with arguments makes him defensive. It's much better to use a digging tool. Questions make him dig down within himself to find out why he's resisting. They lead him to examine his own position to see if it makes sense for him to hold it.

When he's defending himself, he focuses on holding you off. He doesn't consider whether he's making sense. He's too caught up in showing he's right. But when you become his ally, and work with him to reach the right decision, he relaxes and considers the idea more objectively.

To maintain a "working-with" instead of an "against" feeling, you have to think of yourself as helping the other person rather than overcoming him. He's as much a victim of his own unreasonable resistance as you are. Think of yourself as patiently guiding him through his self-imposed obstacles to an objective cost-benefit appraisal of your idea.

The Fear of Looking Foolish

As you persist in the face of the other person's resistance, you risk incurring a greater penalty than losing the sale. For if the other person shows logically that your idea isn't suitable, your persistence makes you seem unreasonable, foolish in fighting for it. Your credibility could be hurt since it might seem as though you just want your way. You might even seem a little dense for not having grasped earlier in the discussion the other person's reasoning against your idea. Or you might seem to be unreasonably resisting her opposing arguments.

You might sense this risk as you fight for your idea. You feel anxious. Part of you wants to withdraw. Should you cut your possible losses by giving up this early in the selling of your idea, or should you take the risk and plunge ahead? If you make the sale, you gain on several counts: Your good idea gets implemented; and you show that you're willing to fight for something you believe in. Both of these enhance your image.

The other person runs the same risks as you do if she prolongs her resistance and then has to concede that your idea is worth using. The fear of looking foolish adds to the fear of angering by persisting. These fears, acting together, mount as the discussion progresses and make it progressively harder to stay with it. Keeping in touch with your fears helps you to control them. Denying or not seeing them allows them to have an exaggerated effect.

Impatience with Listening

Almost all of us use conversation to discharge feelings. We feel burdened by feelings when we hold them in; relieved when we talk them out. As our feelings of fear and anger intensify in the conversation, we want to talk in order to let them out. We don't want to listen.

Another cause of our impatience with listening is our illusion that explaining our logic more clearly will dispel the other person's resistance. It seems as though the only reason he's still resisting is because he hasn't fully grasped our arguments. We want to tell him again. If only he'd stop talking, we'd straighten out his thinking.

When you feel yourself becoming impatient, remind yourself that the other person's talking usually works in your favor. It generally means that he cares, that he is trying to think it through, and that he wants to relate to you. Even when he's explaining his objections, he's getting a better sense of how significant they are. Feelings of resistance, like all feelings, feel larger before they're expressed.

Stresses in Persuading

The persuasive conversation is stressful for both sides. In trying to sell your idea, you're continually beset by emotions surging up within you that you have to control. The body wants to react to anger with fight or flight; and to anxiety and guilt, with either talking it out, or withdrawing. But you have to inhibit these reactions and instead listen closely, think clearly, and talk persuasively.

Similarly, the other person's natural resistance conflicts with his wanting to do the reasonable thing. He also might be made anxious by feeling that he's going to offend you if he rejects your idea, and at the same time knows that he should not allow this to influence his decision. Furthermore, as you continue to present a sound case for your idea, the other person, while pushed by his wanting to resist, finds it harder to justify his opposition. He frantically tries to contrive arguments that have a least some semblance of logic so that he seems at least somewhat reasonable.

As you explain your idea, you wonder anxiously what he's

thinking behind his impassive look. Is he interested in hearing more? Does he think you're talking sensibly? Will he say no? He raises an objection. Objections impose particular stress. Will he listen to your handling of the objection? Will he be unreasonable about it? Questions also impose stress. He asks a question. How well will you answer it?

You're stressed when he interrupts, gets angry, rationalizes, opposes without justifying it, remains silent, or puts off further discussion. You're held in suspense throughout the whole discussion. If the other person turns down your idea, you have to keep reminding yourself that he rejected only your idea, not you. Then there's the stress that comes from the feeling that you're not effective. You're likely to get this feeling if this is the latest of several of your ideas that were turned down one after the other.

People who are low in assertiveness are even more stressed. Not only do they have to contend with the impositions of the other person but they are also frustrated by their own inability to cope with the other person's resistance, and become angry at themselves. And they sell fewer of their ideas, which dampens their job satisfaction and hinders their advancement.

In the following persuasive interaction, "relax" or "calm down" is put at each point of stress for the person selling his idea.

"We ought to make sure our employees know what they're getting in this new, very generous package of benefits we're providing. Each supervisor should have a meeting with his employees to educate them. That way we'll get the full public relations benefit."

"Meetings are too expensive. To have all our employees give up an hour's time would cost far too much. Let's just print up booklets and give one to each employee."

(Relax.) "That would cost less. What good would it do, though, since most of them don't read the booklets that aren't of immediate concern? Most employees read them only when they need a benefit of some kind and wonder what they're entitled to. Meanwhile, they won't appreciate how much they're getting compared to what other firms are giving, and we won't get the advantage of holding on to good employees as well as attracting job applicants."

"They'll read it. People want to know what's coming to them. They even ask about it when they first apply for a job."

(Keep calm.) "Some of them will read, just as some ask about it in the hiring interview. Wouldn't it be greatly to our advantage if *all* of them knew the benefits they're getting, so that they could talk about them and spread the word in the community?"

"Listen, when people get something for nothing, they want to know about it. Everybody loves that."

(Keep cool.) "People like to get something for nothing. Are they really getting the benefits for nothing? Benefits are part of the total compensaion package. Some firms give a little higher wages but less benefits. With our new combination of wages and benefits, we're paying our employees more than other firms in this area."

"Right. That's why they'll want to work for us. It makes sense. We ought to be getting the best people now."

(Relax.) "Yes, we should. But how are we going to get them if all our people won't know about the benefits? And most of them won't know if we give them booklets that they don't read."

"Okay, okay. I see your point. But try to keep the meetings to a half hour."

Being Reasonably Assertive

Being assertive is a critical asset in selling your ideas. It isn't a question of insisting or arguing or demanding. It takes assertiveness just to keep your own anxieties from inhibiting your selling.

The unassertive person is quick to feel he's wrong. When the other person resists, the unassertive person begins to doubt something in what he's doing. He might wonder if his facts or reasoning are right; if he's being honest with himself about his motives; if he's presenting his ideas clearly; if he's doing something that irritates; if the other person considers him presumptuous; and if he's taking up too much time.

It's helpful to view assertiveness not as being able to stand up to the other person's aggressiveness but as being capable of coping with one's own fear of him. Anyone may feel anxious dealing with people who are brusque and domineering. The reasonably assertive person controls her anxiety and, without showing hostility, persists in advancing ideas that she considers reasonable. The unassertive person, when intimidated, is unable to handle her fear and withdraws.

Ironically, her withdrawal encourages the domineering person to continue his intimidation since it "works" with the unassertive one. A person might act out this domineering demeanor as a way of getting the feeling of being an important person. Since it doesn't work for him in the face of reasonable assertiveness, he is likely to abandon it then.

The unassertive person is afraid that his anger will be seen and that he will be punished for it. He views the other person as stronger, and himself as weak. He's angry at this domination of him and afraid that he will act out his anger is some way. So he inhibits his expression generally, submitting or withdrawing.

To break out of this trap, the unassertive person needs to increase her assertiveness in steps small enough so that she can handle her anxiety, doesn't become immobilized. She can start by asking one question about the other person's objection. The next time she might present one piece of contradictory information. The third time she could ask several questions and supply more evidence that argues against the other person's objection. As the unassertive person sees that nothing terrible results from her assertiveness, she feels more confident, and increases it.

Guarding Against Your Own Resistance

Your own resistance can sap your persuasiveness. It's difficult to accept this because none of us feels that he is resistant. This makes your resistance all the more dangerous. It comes disguised as logic or conviction or enthusiasm, and never feels like resistance at all.

Your resistance undermines your credibility. How can the other person have any confidence in your arguments against his objections if he feels that you're motivated by resistance rather than by the facts? As soon as he senses your resistance, he starts to lose interest in the discussion.

Since you won't feel your resistance, you have to step outside yourself and watch your behavior for signs of resistance. One easily observed sign is the immediate rejection of the other person's point. He's hardly finished saying it and you're already denying it's so. You haven't even had time to think about it. This irritates the other person. It makes him feel he's talking to himself. Watch for this premature response in others so that you get used to noticing it.

Another sign of our own resistance is our not listening to the other person's objection. When she voices an objection, we tune it out. We wait for her to stop talking so we can explain our arguments again. We justify ourselves by thinking that we don't have to listen because after her first few words we know what she's going to say. But we can't be sure. And she might add something we didn't expect. Since this should be obvious to us, our not listening means we're resisting.

A good way to counter this in yourself is to ask yourself whether there could be some merit in the other person's objection. Could he mean it differently from the way you're interpreting it? Perhaps he's not saying it clearly. Maybe you'd better ask him to explain it further.

In asking the other person about his objection, you're communicating to him that you're listening closely and weighing each point carefully. Now when you contradict the other person's objection, he's likely to listen more closely. You've become more believable.

Another sign to watch for in yourself is rationalizing to refute the other person's objection. It's more difficult to spot your own false reasoning than to see another person's. The fact that you're using it means that it's already past your own logic censor. You never did look closely since you wanted to get rid of the other person's objection.

We deceive ourselves more easily than we deceive others since in doing so we're serving our own motivations. If a person wants to believe something, any contradictory facts are seldom enlightening. They're just irritating.

While logic is a powerful tool for survival, we still operate to some extent on belief. In an earlier stage in our evolution it might have worked more successfully to decide quickly on belief or habit, than slowly on logic. Biologically, we change very gradually.

A good way to spot our own rationalizing is to put ourselves in the other person's place and to ask ourselves if we'd be convinced by what we're saying. However, we have to watch that we don't answer ourselves too quickly, that we give enough thought to our own question.

|| 12 || How to Have High Credibility

The Skepticism Barrier

People are more skeptical now than ever. They're bombarded daily with an overwhelming amount of information from TV, computers, and innumerable publications. Even if the percentage that's false hasn't changed, there's a lot more false information just because there's much more information.

False information affects credibility much more than true information does. When people get a piece of false information, it lowers their confidence in the source of that information far more than getting true information raises it. Getting false information jars them. They remember it with a feeling of being deceived or being treated carelessly. Getting true information they take for granted.

Since people keep getting more false information, they keep getting more distrustful. They consider false or suspect, also, information that contradicts their viewpoints. Information supporting a politically conservative recommendation is generally considered suspect by a liberal and vice versa. Facts that contradict religious beliefs are rejected as false by the believer. Two people who have different backgrounds, and know from experience that these different backgrounds generally result in different attitudes, have lower credibility for each other. Each is skeptical about the other's information.

When you impart information to someone who doesn't know you, you start at a credibility disadvantage. You have no credibility history with him, but people in general do. And people in general have given him a mixture of true and false information. Therefore, the information you give him could be either. He remains skeptical. The burden of proof rests with you.

Generally, people express only a small portion of their skepticism. They feel that to ask for justification of every assertion is to question the other person's integrity and competence. They do this mostly when it can appear to be a seeking of better understanding rather than an expression of distrust.

To illuminate the extent of the receiver's skepticism, he expresses it all in the conversation that follows:

"The purchasing agent at National called yesterday and said that stuff we shipped them three days ago is giving them trouble in production. I checked the run and everything's okay, so they must be using it wrongly, or something looks wrong to them that isn't. We'd better send a tech service man out there to look into it."

"How did you check the run?"

"I looked at the test data that the inspector entered in the log for the sample he took from the run."

"Is the inspector new? Maybe he didn't know what he was doing."

"No, he's an old-timer and reliable."

"How do you know he's the one who measured the sample? If the inspector's not around at the moment and they can't wait, often someone else steps in and does it for him, even using his initials to cover for him."

"No, it was him. I talked to him and I know him well enough to know he wouldn't lie to me."

"Some contamination might have happened in the warehouse or somewhere in shipping."

"I called the other customers who got shipments from that run and none of them had any complaints."

"Maybe none of them used it yet."

"No, I asked about that and two did use it and it was fine."

"Okay, send someone out."

The Importance of Credibility to Selling Ideas

How can someone buy an idea if he doesn't feel confident that the presented facts are true? Also, even if he cross-examines on the reasoning and on the source of the facts, he can't be sure that he's not overlooking something. He might have slipped up on asking about some jumped-to conclusion. He needs to rely on the presenter's concern for the truth to supplement his own.

Talking about "high" and "low" credibility is misleading since it implies that there is a scale of credibility. It's as though a person could have any degree of credibility. For all practical purposes there is no scale. A person either has credibility or he doesn't. For how useful is it to say that someone has moderate credibility? Would you make a decision on the basis of his information, or pass it along for someone else's use?

If a person is right half the time and wrong half the time, is his credibility fifty percent? No, it's zero in a practical sense. For you can't do anything useful with the information he gives you. You know there's a fifty percent chance that what he now says is true. But how can you use that except to place a bet if you like to gamble?

Having credibility is essential to get the other person to listen in the first place. If you have no credibility, he won't even consider your idea. But even if the other person has the highest confidence in your credibility, he still wants to examine your facts and reasoning.

Having credibility doesn't mean that what you say is true. It means that you don't lie and that you try hard to avoid error. But you can try hard and still make a mistake. Perhaps your conclusion was wrong because you didn't take into account certain facts that you couldn't have known about. Or suppose you get some of your facts from a credible source, whether a person or a publication, that made a mistake. Everyone makes mistakes.

Yet many people are somewhat offended when you ask how they arrived at a conclusion. They feel that you're questioning their credibility. They overlook the error factor. Perhaps down deep they feel that making any error is a sign of incompetence, as though all errors were preventable. Here we have a feeling that's in conflict with reality.

Still, we all have a certain amount of insecurity that causes us to continually measure ourselves. Since there are no absolute standards for measuring such characteristics as our competence, credibility, kindness, courage, or effect on people, we can do so only by comparing ourselves with others and from the feedback we get from them.

When you question someone about the basis for his conclusion, he might feel that his competence and credibility are being questioned. His insecurity blocks him from considering that you might be checking only for error. Your questioning becomes for him negative feedback, which could irritate him and make him defensive. His irritation becomes feedback to you about your effect on people, and can make you anxious, or irritated with him.

A good way to avoid the unpleasant feelings on both sides that could come from your being questioned about your conclusions is to tell the basis of your conclusions. However, you'll still need to question the other person if he doesn't give his basis, and you disagree with his conclusions. To minimize the interplay of negative feelings, you can explain that you're asking to get a better understanding of his thinking, to make sure that you don't form any wrong conclusions.

Losing Credibility Without Realizing It

We tend to underestimate the effects our false information has on others. Many of us feel that if the information is unimportant, it doesn't affect credibility. If there are no consequences that matter, why would anyone remember the false information?

People remember it because they're always trying to figure out how reliable any piece of information is that affects them in any way. One important indicator is the credibility of the source of the information. And the way we evaluate a source's credibility is to consider the accuracy of all the information we've received from the source.

If a person claims that he lies only in unimportant matters, how do we know what other criteria he might be using to justify his lying? He might feel that if he gains enough, or if no one is hurt, or if he makes someone feel good, that justifies it. Furthermore, what does he mean by "unimportant" or "hurt?" Your communicating just one small piece of false information causes others to wonder how much of the rest is false.

To have credibility, you have to adopt as a principle communicating only true information. This means using information from only credible sources. If you're unsure, check it out. Think very carefully about it before lying. If you're caught, the price you pay in credibility loss is incredibly high. Generally, it's not worth it.

The trouble is that we kid ourselves too easily when we're under stress. Under the stress of wanting to sell our idea we might stretch the truth a bit. We might exaggerate the benefits and minimize the obstacles and the risk. If the other person finds out, we lose credibility even if the idea succeeds. We were just lucky we beat the odds. The next time he won't be able to count on our facts' being true, and he knows that we might not be so lucky then.

In a hiring interview I conducted with an applicant for a job with a client company, the applicant said that he had attended college for four years but didn't get a degree. When I questioned him further, it turned out that he actually attended for only three and a half years. When I asked him why he claimed four years, he replied that he always said four years and didn't think it mattered. But I found myself wondering at that moment whether the three and a half years was so, whether he actually went to that college, and if his dates of employment at his past jobs were true.

Whether it be to gain some personal end or to have the pleasure of being helpful to someone, people give information they don't know is true as though they were certain of it. Often, they don't face that they don't know until you ask them if they're sure. At times, people give travel directions that are wrong, tell the wrong time that a store closes, supply the population size of a town when they don't know it, and convey all kinds of other misinformation. When a person does this, her credibility goes down the drain with those who get to know her. They may like her for other reasons but they simply stop believing her.

The person who gives wrong information repeatedly is generally unaware of its effect on others, and often doesn't realize that his information is wrong. It seems right to him. He doesn't think further about the degree of confidence he has in the information he's giving. He's not motivated to think about it because he doesn't realize how much he loses in credibility when he communicates even the most innocuous piece of wrong information.

No matter how insignificant the information seems, before giving it ask yourself how sure you are about it. If you're not sure, either say so or don't give it, depending on how unsure you are. If you lack some confidence in the source of the information, tell what the source is.

Easy Ways to Lose Credibility

When you lie to one person in front of a second, and the second person knows you're lying, you lose credibility with him. Even if he understands your reason for lying and can sympathize with it, his confidence in what you say is diminished. If your child hears you tell someone that you're sick, because you want to get out of doing something, you lose credibility with your child. He comes to realize that you're not scrupulous about the truth. Since you're a model for him, he may even start doing the same thing.

When you falsely deny others' claims that you have certain faults, or that you caused something to go wrong, you lose credibility with them whether you're lying just to them, or to yourself also. How far will you go with your wishful thinking? However, if you recognize that you could be kidding yourself, and after an initial disagreement you ask the other person for the basis of her thinking, and really compare her reasoning with yours, and go by the weight of the evidence, you maintain credibility. We all do some wishful thinking. What's important is your willingness to consider that you might be doing it.

When you make either a factual or a reasoning error, you lose credibility. If you're trying to sell an idea and the other person discovers an error somewhere in your presentation, she wonders where else there might be an error. You might say, But we all make mistakes. Shouldn't allowances be made for that? What if I tripped and fell, or added a column of figures wrong, or didn't see a misspelled word? I don't lose credibility from any of these errors.

That's true, but the difference between this kind of error

and a factual or reasoning error lies in whether you could be motivated to make the error. Making a factual or reasoning error might serve your purpose. Furthermore, you can't control making a typing error or not discovering it; nor can you control accidentally dropping a glass. But you can control the information you give out. You can't control someone's misinforming you but you can control checking the information.

If you have control, your motivation affects what you do. When motivation comes into play, people attribute motivations to you if your motivation isn't apparent. If you misinform with information that favors your position, they're likely to feel that you deliberately misinformed. This lowers your credibility.

If your misinformation argues against your position, it's less likely to hurt your credibility. But those who are characteristically suspicious still may feel that you have something to gain by it but they don't know what it is. Or they may contrive motivation such as that you didn't really want to sell your idea, because it would cause you more work or lower your budget, but you wanted to show that you're willing to advance an idea that's good for the organization even though it's bad for you. However, hardly anyone has credibility with the characteristically suspicious, anyway.

You're responsible for managing your information. Managing it means making sure it's true. If you can't manage it, whether because you're inept at doing so or because you can't resist manipulating it to serve your purposes, you will lose credibility.

How Resistance to Ideas
Lowers Credibility

Since we all have resistance to others' ideas, if we can't reject an idea reasonably, we turn to unreasonable ways. We rationalize, become irrelevant, change the subject, nitpick, or get angry. As soon as we become unreasonable, we lose credibility. If we can't manage our resistance, we can't manage information.

Avoiding loss of credibility, as well as loss of good ideas, is another good reason for keeping our resistance down. When you listen carefully, ask for more information, and weigh the evidence on both sides, your credibility is maintained. It shows you want to make the decision that follows realistically from the way things are.

People are so transparent in their resistance that it's a wonder they don't see it in themselves. The ability to deceive ourselves is apparently very well developed. But then we meet ourselves halfway. We're both the needy con artist and the willing victim. And in playing out this self-deception we're much less inscrutable to others than we think.

How to Evaluate Your Credibility

Your credibility with a particular individual depends on how well he knows you. If he hardly knows you, your credibility depends on his habitual skepticism and on how well you support your conclusions with evidence. If he knows you, your credibility depends on how truthfully you informed him in the past.

To evaluate your own credibility, you have to watch the people who know you. Ask yourself the following: When people talk with you, do they seem interested in discussing your ideas with you, or do they try to evade it? Do they focus their questions more on getting further information, or do they mainly ask how you arrived at particular conclusions or how you know certain facts are so?

Some people are more skeptical than others are. The skeptics question the basis of almost all conclusions. It doesn't mean that your credibility is low if a skeptic cross-examines you. You would have to get the reactions of several people of varying skepticism to get a useful appraisal.

As a check on yourself, watch for how often you make assertions without having support for them. It would be helpful to ask yourself beforehand, What would I say if the other person asks me what I base my assertion on? A further check is to ask yourself, If someone else said that to me, would I be convinced?

Let's listen to a salesperson losing credibility as she talks to her boss.

"Meg, what's the problem with Universal? Why aren't we getting business there?"

"Our price is too high. We've got to come down some. I think I could get in there if we were about five percent lower."

"What makes you think that?"

"Well, it's got to be price. We're competitive in every other way—quality, service, delivery—so I figure it must be price."

"Maybe the buyer and the salesperson are good buddies, or the salesperson's doing a big entertaining job."

"It couldn't be that. I know the salesperson. He's not big on personality."

"But does that mean there couldn't be good chemistry between them?"

"There could be, but this buyer's not a quiet type."

"They used to use our product until they had some trouble with it. We made some bad shipments. Maybe it's that."

"It couldn't be. That problem we had was in quality control, and we cleared that up a while back. It's got to be price."

"But the buyer hasn't bought anything from us since then. Maybe she's not convinced."

"Just let me go in at five percent less and I'll get the business. I know this buyer. She buys on price."

"What makes you say that? She's buying from Consolidated now. They're not the lowest-priced supplier. In fact, our price is generally about the same as theirs. Go back in there and try to get the true story. Talk to some other people in the company."

"How come you don't believe me?"

"Because I go by the facts and you haven't given me any; and because you do this a lot, making claims and not backing them up. What do you think this does to your credibility? Suppose I evaluated your performance that way—no facts, just my feelings. Would that convince you?"

"I see what you mean. But I know how to read these buyers. I know the signs."

"There you go again. How'd you like it if people called you no-facts Meg? Keep that in mind. It might help you remember to have the facts ready when you talk to me, to your customers and prospects, and anyone."

"Do I really talk with no facts? I didn't realize it. Watch me from now on. I'll make a solid case. Thanks for your help."

How to Build and Maintain Credibility

Since credibility can seep away through even small cracks in the truth, it's helpful to be forthright and direct. View your interaction as though the burden rests on you to prove that you're truthful rather than on the other person to catch you deceiving him. The reason for doing this is the common tendency to attribute self-serving motivations to others. If what you're saying could be interpreted either way, the chances are the other person will suspect you're slanting your story to gain something.

If your mind wanders for the moment and you don't answer the other person's question, he's likely to assume that you're evading it. If something unfavorable about your idea emerges in response to a question he asks before you could tell him about it on your own initiative, he'll assume you weren't going to tell him about it. And often he might very well feel that your errors aren't accidental if they favor your idea, but represent wishful thinking.

This doesn't mean that you have to bring up every doubt you have about your idea, or clutter up your discussion with qualifications of everything you say. If you do this, you'll be communicating that you have little confidence in your own idea.

To maintain your credibility you need to do the following:

(a) maintain a mind-set of wanting to work out with the other person what is the most gainful thing for the both of you to do about your idea, rather than just thinking of selling it to him;

(b) tell what you base your conclusions on and the sources of your information;

(c) look into objections instead of immediately trying to refute them;

(d) answer all questions straightforwardly, and if you don't know the answer, say so rather than trying to contrive one.

If you differ from the other person in your attitudes and values, whether about politics or religion, or you have different backgrounds, it's better not to draw attention to the differences when you're trying to sell your idea. These kinds of differences lower each person's credibility for the other even though the differences have no bearing on the idea.

When you have something to gain personally if the other person buys your idea, your credibility is lower than it is for someone who is seen as having nothing at stake personally. Regarding the purchase of an office machine, the office manager's recommendation has more credibility than the sales representative's.

A person may have credibility in some areas of information

and lack credibility in others. When a woman asks her husband, "How do I look?" after she dresses up to go to a party, she is really asking, "How will I look to others?" If he replies that she looks great, and this is his usual response, she's likely to say, with some irritation, "You always say that."

The husband, who then wonders how his wife could be displeased with that, doesn't realize that she feels she can't rely on him to tell her how others will see her. She knows that she can't always be looking great, which means to her that her husband doesn't see the flaws when she's not up to par. Her husband doesn't have credibility in this area.

On visiting my mother, she asked me how I felt. I replied, "Fine." She complained, "You always tell me that." For the moment, it seemed as though she preferred me to say I feel bad. I figured that perhaps she wanted a chance to talk to me about my health. However, on reflection, I realized that she was frustrated because she thought I was concealing how I really felt. She knew I couldn't always be feeling fine, so my continually saying it in response meant to her that I was misinforming her. To her, my credibility wasn't there on this particular topic.

People continually look for cues to the credibility of information as they're receiving it. Does the person telling it hesitate? Is he vague in explaining things? Does he leave out things? Does he contradict himself? Is he exaggerating? For example:

"Henry is spending his money wildly."

"What do you mean?"

"He just bought an expensive new car. He needed a new car but he didn't need that kind of luxury."

"So what if he indulged himself with a car. He loves cars. Does that mean he's spending his money wildly on everything?"

"If he does it with one thing, he'll do it with others. That's the way people are."

Emotional excitement can lower credibility. When you're making a case, it's better to be calm and dispassionate. A person's being emotional about his position suggests that he might not be seeing things clearly. Certainly, enthusiasm is a plus, but only if it's backed up with evidence. It's not the enthusiasm but the evidence that makes for credibility. Anger arouses skepticism. In arguing against something, whether orally or in writing, try to present your logic in a reasoned tone so that the other person doesn't figure that you're exaggerating to discharge anger about something else that's bothering you.

Having a reputation for telling the truth, getting facts, reasoning carefully so that your conclusions are justified, and deciding from the evidence rather than from your wishes is invaluable. It gets people to listen and to want to know more. And they're much less likely to look for holes. Keep in mind that when you're wrong, you can lose more credibility from denying it than from being wrong.

‖13‖ How to Negotiate Effectively

The Conflict Between Being Fair and Getting the Most

To negotiate effectively, you have to sell a number of ideas. When you want to maintain a continuing relationship, it's essential that you're able to justify the deal you're offering as reasonably fair. You've got to sell the other person on seeing as fair what you consider as being fair. You may lose more by hurting the relationship than you gain from getting more than you deserve. Getting too much may also make you feel guilty, as well as anxious that the other person is angry at you for it. The effect on the relationship and the feelings aroused on both sides have to be weighed in order to get at the true terms of the deal.

    To sell the fairness of the deal, you have to sell the other person out of his overvaluing what he's giving up, and undervaluing what he's gaining. This becomes more difficult when he's motivated to get the most he can in return for giving up the least he has to. Getting the most for the least might give him a feeling of being powerful and competent. This may mean more to him than does the feeling of being honest and considerate.

When we negotiate, we're frequently placed in an inner conflict between our wanting to win, and our common drive to achieve equity. We get an additional push toward striving for the most by the feeling that the other person's doing it so why shouldn't we? We're afraid we might feel like a fool if we don't. And we don't want to feel angry because we get too little, or guilty because we got too much.

To negotiate successfully and maintain a good relationship, you need to enlist the other person's drives toward being both reasonable and fair. To do this, you have to disarm him by your trying to be that way. You've got to set aside any fear you have that he might take advantage of you. Keep in mind that you control what you're willing to give up. If you start by asking for too much, the other person immediately senses that you're seeking the most for the least rather than a fair deal.

How to Use People's Desire
to be Fair

To support the other person's drive toward reasonableness, you have to appeal to reason. This means supporting with logic what you're proposing. You have to have evidence and rationales. If you're selling something that's subject to negotiating, you have to explain why it's worth what you're asking. If you're the buyer and you offer a lower price than the seller is asking, justify your lower price. Don't just trade numbers.

Let's watch a job candidate negotiate his salary in the hiring interview. The interview is at the point of discussing this subject.

"I see from your application that you're asking for $40,000 in salary. That's more than we figured on. We had in mind $34,000 as a starting salary."

"I was making $38,000 in my last job but performing at a

level that justified much more. I introduced procedures that saved twenty worker-hours a week, which was worth $10,000 a year to the company. Also, I developed a training method that enabled us to hire people with less education for particular tasks. As a result, we saved $20,000 a year on salaries. This was in addition to carrying out my regular duties. Wouldn't it be well worth it for you to go a little higher if you could expect to get back much more in return?"

"Well, we might go to $36,000 to start and if you work out as well as you seem to expect, we could perhaps raise you to $40,000 in a year."

"That sounds reasonable. But why would you need to wait a year to find out, when I've done this kind of job before? I thought it might be justified to raise me in steps to $38,000 in six months if you're happy with me, and on to $40,000 after a year."

"Well, even if we did go in six-month steps, we might feel after six months that your performance deserves a raise to only $37,000 or no raise at all. Rather than committing ourselves, we'd want to play it as it goes."

"Yes, that does make sense. Does that mean then after six months, if I did exceptionally well, I'd be raised to more than $38,000? It seems to me that if we have flexibility to go lower, we should have it to go higher, as well."

"I guess we can manage that. It seems to me that when you get a good idea, you're somehow going to negotiate it into action."

Negotiating to Get the Most for the Least

Let's suppose that in a particular negotiation you aren't concerned with a long-term relationship. Also, you don't care about being fair. You just want to get the best deal you can. Both sides want the deal to go through or else they wouldn't be negotiating. And the deal will go through if the range that's acceptable to one side overlaps the range that's acceptable to the other. However, up until the point of agreement, each side wants to make it appear as though the other side's offer is unacceptable. For each side is trying to get the other to keep raising its offer until its maximum is reached. And each side feels the other is doing the same.

This mutual suspicion means that neither side has credibility with the other. What one says, the other doesn't believe. Every remark is aimed at getting the other side to agree to whatever the remark proposes; or failing that, to reveal more about the other side's maximums and minimums.

Listen to this:

"So how much will you charge to do the job?"

"It's a big job, takes a lot of paint. And there are tricky places that eat up a lot of time. I'd have to charge five thousand dollars, and that's very little for this kind of a job."

"Five thousand dollars! You've got to be kidding. We're talking about a house not a stadium. Maybe you thought I meant both outside and inside. I just want the outside."

"I couldn't go below five thousand. And I had to do a lot of figuring to get it down to that. Paint is very high and my painters get a lot of money, and I've got to take responsibility. I can't cut corners."

"I'll give you thirty-five hundred and you can start tomorrow. It's getting cold out. There won't be many painting days left. And if I see you're a good painter with reasonable prices, I could be giving you other jobs and recommending you around."

"Maybe I could drop it a few hundred to forty-five hundred. That really pushes me to the wall. I'll probably end up losing money. But that's it. Take it or leave it."

"I discovered a secret. The painting business is the way to get rich. If I charged my customers that kind of price, I'd have such a big house that forty-five hundred would be a cheap price.

But maybe you've got the right idea. Make it in a hurry and then take it easy. No hustle or hassle. I'll tell you what, just to make sure you don't have to cut any corners and can use the best of everything, I'll give you four thousand. That's my last offer because much as I enjoy talking with you I've got too many other things to do."

"You're right. We're wasting time. I'll do it for forty-three hundred, and let me go to work. The sooner I start, the sooner you'll have the best-looking house in the neighborhood."

"Okay, okay, why should we keep trying to take each other's money? Do it for forty-three hundred but throw in the deck. It's a small deck."

"I wish I had a deck that size. You must give some big parties, which I couldn't afford to do, anyway. If I had to throw in the deck, I might as well throw in the towel. But I tell you what, I'll throw in the fence. I shouldn't but I will. Now, let me get started."

"You got a deal, but remember, only the best paint."

"The best paint is all I use."

Finding Out Maximums and Minimums

The most valuable piece of information you can uncover is the maximum the other side will give up, or the minimum he will accept for what he gives up. If you know this, you just have to hold out.

However, the other side is aware of this, too, and is trying to find out your maximum or minimum while concealing his. This turns the negotiating into a poker game with each side bluffing the other until one gives way. The risk comes in going too far and causing the collapse of the negotiation.

Let's say that you want to find out the other side's minimum. Both of you start some distance apart and move toward each other. At the start, you're offering less and he's asking more than either of you expects the other to accept. Before you start, work out the point at which you feel the deal would be fair to both sides. His minimum is likely to lie somewhere between your starting point and the fairness point. Then, at a point about midway between your starting point and the fairness point, begin testing to find the other side's minimum.

While you can test by simply declaring that this is as far as you can go, you run the risk that the other side will end the negotiating by saying he can't accept your offer and there's no point in going on. He may really mean this, or he may just be testing to see if you mean to stop. If you then increase your offer, you've lost your credibility while his remains intact. The next time you refuse to go further, he's likely to threaten to withdraw as a way of getting you to increase your offer.

On the other hand, if you decide to hold fast, as a way of testing to see if he's bluffing, you place him in the position of having to lose face as well as credibility if he wants to continue the negotiation. For to do so, he has to back away from a position he declared is firm. Depending on his character, this might make the deal too costly for him, even if he were willing to give up more tangibles.

A more subtle and less risky way of testing at that same midway point is to increase your resistance to moving further but not say you won't. You can use both of the following methods simultaneously to do so: 1. step up the amount of arguing you do in support of each succeeding offer you make; and 2. reduce the size of your steps toward him.

These signal him that you're not cutting off further movement but that you're getting close to the maximum you'll give up. It means also that he has to work harder for each bit of movement that he gets from you. In addition, it makes him feel that he's running the risk of overstepping your maximum; and if that happens, he'll either lose the deal or he'll lose face by having to back away from his last demand. He may feel that it's not worth the risk to keep pushing for what little more he might be able to get.

You're not cut off even if you underestimate the gap between the both of you, and you resist too strongly. Let's say he declares he wants to cut off the negotiation. You can still keep it moving without losing credibility since you never stopped, never drew any line. You can ask him how far apart do the two of you seem, and why not keep going in order to reach a deal?

Let's watch the prospective buyer of a used car apply this method:

"Thirty-four hundred dollars is way too high for a car this old. I had in mind twenty-six hundred."

The buyer, to get the car for as little as he can, tries to set a low center point between himself and the seller. He starts well below both the maximum he's willing to pay, which is thirty-two hundred dollars, and what he considers a fair price: three thousand dollars. At the same time, because he doesn't want the seller to withdraw, he signals his willingness to move by telling what he "had in mind" (past tense) rather than what he will give (future tense).

Also, he doesn't put pressure behind his figure by arguing for it.

"You're way out of the ball park. This car is in good shape, looks good, and doesn't have that much mileage on it. I'm not saying I can't be a little flexible. I might drop it down a hundred or so if you're ready to buy."

"The car is old, which means a lot of things can go wrong with it. But it fits some particular needs of mine so I'll give you twenty-seven fifty."

The buyer puts a little pressure behind his offer by saying the car is old. At the same time he disarms by conveying reasonableness in telling something favorable.

"I couldn't even consider twenty-seven fifty. But if you're

willing to write out a check now, I'll let you have it for thirty-one hundred."

"Look, there are dents in the body, the tires are retreads, there's no telling what the mileage is, the upholstery is worn, and there are scratches in the windshield. Even though the car suits my purposes, I can only go so high. I'll give you twenty-eight fifty."

The buyer has stepped up his pressure and shortened his step toward the seller, but he hasn't drawn a line.

"We're not getting anywhere. We're too far apart. There's not enough give to close the gap."

"How far apart do you think we really are?"

"I don't know where you are but I can't go much more."

"Okay, I'll go fifty more, but that's damn risky. There could be nine hundred other things wrong with the car that I'll suffer with afterwards."

"There's nothing wrong with this car. Make it a hundred more and we'll deal. And it's probably the best deal you've made in a long time."

"Let's split the difference at twenty-nine twenty-five, and I'll write the check."

"All right. Let's get it over with."

Offering and Counteroffering

When you're concerned about maintaining a good relationship, your aim in negotiating is to make the deal fair to both sides, rather than to get the most for the least. If you get more than you should, which means the other person gets less than she deserves, you're likely to anger her. This may cost you more in the long run than you gained in this negotiation.

Your perception of what's fair may differ from the other person's. Another complication is that you may want to maintain the relationship more than she does. Also, you may want to bring about a deal more than she does.

These differences mean that negotiating where you care about keeping up the relationship calls for continuous selling. You may have to sell the following ideas: that what you're proposing is fair; that maintaining the relationship is a greater benefit than she realizes; and that she has more to gain from making a deal with you than she recognizes.

Beyond that you have to sell the fairness of all your offers and counteroffers. If you don't justify them, it seems as though your guiding principle is to get the most for the least. Giving this impression hurts the relationship. For it means that you're willing to deprive the other person of what she should have. But if achieving fairness is what guides you, she feels she can trust you since you then are concerned about her interests as well as yours. To maintain your credibility, your initial offer must be fairly close to your terms for settlement. If you finally accept much less than your initial request, the other person is likely to think that you are trying to get much more than is reasonable. In future negotiations, she'll distrust your first offer and feel that she has to keep bargaining with you just to get terms that are fair.

When you make an offer, you have to show why the other person is gaining the equivalent of what he's giving up. And when you reject his offer as being insufficient, and come back with a counteroffer that gives him less, you need to demonstrate that your counteroffer comes closer to an equal gain for both than his offer does.

To demonstrate the fairness of your offers and counteroffers, give evidence to support them. In rejecting an offer, treat it as though it were an objection. This means using a constructive inquiry or a reasoning one, asking him to show how you're getting in return as much value as he is.

Let's observe two self-employed consultants, Donna and

Tim, negotiate the proportion of the overhead each is to pay for a suite of offices they plan to share. They are not business partners. The overhead includes rent, salary for a secretary-receptionist, the shared portion of the telephone system, and any other equipment and supplies they use jointly. Donna uses the inquiry method.

"It seems to me, Tim, that you should pay two-thirds, and I one-third, of the overhead expenses. This is about the way the use of everything is likely to divide since you do twice as much business as I do."

"That doesn't seem fair, Donna. Your office is almost the same size as mine."

"My office is almost the same size. What if we take into account all the values of an office instead of just the size? Your office has a more imposing location, being in a corner and farther away from the receptionist; and being in a corner gives it a better view with its two exposures and broader vista. Also, it's quieter since it's farther from the secretary-receptionist." (Donna uses a constructive inquiry to suggest a different way to look at the situation.)

"That's true, but it doesn't make my office worth twice as much as yours. Size is still the primary factor. View, location, and quietness are worth less."

"Yes, individually they're worth less than the space. But how about when all three are added together? To see it more clearly, if we exchanged offices, what proportion would you expect me to pay?" (She uses an inquiry into reasoning that includes a role reversal.)

"I don't know, Donna. I haven't thought about it. I would expect you to pay more but I don't know that it would be twice as much."

"Would what you'd expect me to pay be closer to two-thirds to one-third, than it would be to fifty-fifty?"

"Maybe a little closer. But the other parts of overhead should be fifty-fifty since you might very well wind up using them as much as or more than I do. You might use the phone and secretary and other things to pursue new business to a greater extent than I do, even though I'm doing more business now."

"You're right, Tim, I could increase my use. Why don't we work out a reasonable estimate of how much each of us is likely to use the overhead items now, apart from our own offices. Then if my use increases we can adjust the proportions." (A constructive inquiry.)

"What do you have in mind?"

"Well, since we each do our own selling, which takes about a quarter of our time, let's say we both use the office setup about equally to get new business. However, I figure you use the setup about twice as much to service your present business since you do twice as much business. You're able to do twice as much by farming out a lot of the work to free-lancers. But you still have to have twice as much contact with your clients and your free-lancers as I do, which means twice the phone calls and correspondence. Let's combine one-quarter of our time at fifty-fifty with three-quarters at two-thirds to one-third. This comes to your using sixty-two and a half percent to my thirty-seven and a half percent. Considering the advantages of your office over mine, I figure it comes closer to two-thirds to one-third."

"That seems a little off to me, Donna, but it's close. Tell you what. I'll go along with my five to your three."

"It's a deal."

The Stresses in Negotiating

Negotiating is stressful since it's essentially adversarial. It can arouse all kinds of uncomfortable feelings: anxiety about losing, both from getting unfavorable terms and from loss of face and of a feeling of incompetence if the negotiating is not done successfully; guilt about possibly asking for more than one deserves; fear of angering the other person; and conflict over wanting to get more versus striving for fairness.

There are also the stresses of uncertainty over both what the other side's next move will be, and what outcome will result. A decision has to be made about how to respond to each change in the situation, and each decision carries risk. Another stress comes from the need to conceal your feelings. If you show eagerness, anxiety, conflict, or guilt, the other side may try to exploit it by presenting a firmer stance than he really feels. You have to be guarded, which may not be natural for you. And you can find yourself continually wondering, Did I tip my hand? How will he interpret what I said? Did I sound firmer or more flexible than I meant to convey?

If the other side is adept at manipulating through intimidation, he may bring your self-doubt into play by making you feel unreasonable and greedy, and himself seem open and fair-minded, when the opposite could be the case. He might say, "Getting this settled fairly is going to require both of us to be reasonable and to look at the other side. We can't let greed take over." It sounds as though he's being reasonable and needs to remind you to be so, also.

The Driving Force of Principles

Principles play a role in all negotiating. In some cases they play the dominant role, and it's the principles that are being negotiated. One such principle might cover who decides what. Does management or the union decide how many people are required to perform a certain task? Another principle might be that the same terms should apply as are generally prevailing in similar situations. This means that you'd expect to earn the same as others do in similar jobs, or buy or sell a house for what other similar houses are costing.

Other principles are: If you had a certain right to do something, and are willing to give it up, you should get something in return; if you're injured, compensation should be in proportion to that injury; and if you invested something, your return should be adjusted to the risk you're taking.

Principles are often rooted in deeper, more fundamental principles. The union's principle that it should decide the number of people to do a job might be based on the principle that people have a right to make decisions that affect their health and safety.

Principles often conflict with each other. The principle that the punishment should fit the crime, based on the Old Testament principle of an eye for an eye, may come up against the principle that there shall be no cruel or inhuman punishment, such as occurs when prisons are overcrowded.

A nation's government may negotiate on the principle that it has the sovereign right to decide who shall enter its land. In so doing, it might come in conflict with its neighboring country's principle that it has the right to pursue terrorists across the border in order to protect its secruity. The principle that guarantees freedom of speech can conflict with the one forbidding incitement to violence.

Even a straightforward negotiation of the price for a particular item can involve a conflict of principle: On the one hand, the value of what's paid should be equal to the value received; and on the other hand, one should get the best deal he can.

In negotiating, try to identify the other person's principles as they come up, and be conscious of your own. Bring out the other person's by using an inquiry into his reasoning that supports a particular offer or demand. Once both sides' principles are brought out, compromises can be constructively worked out. Explore the other person's reasoning in applying the principle. To what extent is it relevant to this case? Are there contradictory principles that also have to be accommodated? This is illustrated in the next section.

Negotiating with Someone
on the Same Side

When you negotiate with your boss about implementing your idea for increasing the organization's effectiveness, the situation is somewhat different from that of selling a house or reaching agreement on a contract. With a house or a contract, one's greater gain is the other's greater loss.

At first glance, you might ask, Why do you have to negotiate with the boss? If your idea is good, you both gain; if it's bad, you both lose. Wouldn't you just work out together whether to act on the idea? Yes, you would do that, but it goes further. The ways of acting on the idea affect him and you differently.

While both of you gain if the idea works, your motivations are different. You gain only if your idea is accepted and then succeeds. Your boss gains if any of the ideas presented to him succeeds. You're concerned with only getting part of his resources allocated to your idea. He wants to distribute his resources over the mix of ideas that will net him the best return. If he invests in your idea and it doesn't work, it means that he's likely lost out on another idea, as well. For if he had more ideas to try than his resources could support, he had to give up another promising idea to try yours.

Since you gain only from your idea, you're motivated to get all the resources you need to maximize the chance that your idea will work. Your boss, on the other hand, wants to minimize his loss if your idea doesn't work. Therefore, he wants to commit only as much as he has to in order to give it a fair chance of working. Often, you and he have to negotiate how much to commit since your perception and his of what's needed might very well be different.

Let's say that a certain minimum investment is needed to give your idea any chance of success; and beyond that, the greater the investment, the greater the chance of success up to some point. With each further investment, the increase in the chance of success keeps getting smaller and smaller until a still further investment makes hardly any difference. You're likely to feel that the investment to make is the one that gives the idea the greatest chance of success, even though you're at the point where the curve of return on investment is starting to flatten out. He may continue only as long as the curve is still rising sharply.

You and he are likely to negotiate not only how much chance of success to give the idea but also how much chance it has for each amount of investment. After all, these are only estimates motivated by differing concerns.

Your wanting to sell your idea might cause you to underestimate the risk, while his concern for preserving his resources could cause him to overestimate it. Generally, neither of you can pinpoint the true risk, nor the optimum amount of resources to commit. You wind up negotiating this, depending on the kind of relationship you have.

The conflict in viewpoints between you and your boss is further complicated by both your and his internal conflicts. On the one hand, you want to sell your idea and get the most commitment you can; on the other hand, you're afraid that in your eagerness you might misrepresent, sell something unwise, and feel guilty as well as lose credibility. Your boss wants to profit from a good idea, maintain a good relationship with you, and encourage you to contribute good ideas, but he also wants to allocate his resources for the best return and keep himself looking and feeling competent.

Let's watch a manager of human resources negotiating with her boss.

"If we were to market to other companies three excellent training programs that our training department developed for our own employees, we'd get back the development cost and make a profit. We could put this money into developing and selling other programs. This could be done with a start-up budget of fifty thousand for the first year—for advertising, for shaping these programs into marketable packages, and for a half-time person to run this activity. After the first year, it should be self-supporting and moving toward returning a profit."

"Your idea would make sense if we were in the education business, but we're not. Our business is completely different, and we ought to concentrate on making it better."

The boss's objection is based on a principle: One should stick to one's business. Since principles are strong motivators, the manager, in her next remark, deals with the principle directly rather than amplifying her original argument. Note how she asks about other contradictory principles that the boss also follows.

"The education business is different from what we're doing now. But doesn't our business now have a number of diverse products that are different from the ones we started with, and that go into different markets? Wouldn't we be doing what we're doing with our other products: Trying to get a good return on investment?"

"But we don't know anything about the education business. That's when it becomes risky, when you invest in something you're ignorant about."

The boss again argues from a principle. The manager stays with the principle, trying to fit under it.

"That's right. It is risky to put money where you're ignorant. But in a way, haven't we been somewhat in the education business? We've been developing successful training programs and marketing them to our own employees. Department heads are not under any obligation to use our programs for their people, and we charge them when they do. Yet they're supporting our programs and are particularly enthusiastic about these three programs. They've used them for a lot of their people. Other companies are going to want these programs, too."

"Well, the idea might be okay in principle, but I couldn't possibly budget fifty thousand dollars for it. We've got too many other pressing needs."

While it might be tempting to ask the boss how much he could spend, it would only increase his resistance since he doesn't know enough about the project to commit a particular amount. Another losing tactic is to drop your cost down to your minimum all at once. If you do, you'll lose credibility. The boss will wonder why you asked for fifty thousand without even offering your minimum as an option.

"It is a lot of money. What if I cut it to thirty-five thousand by reducing the advertising, and packaging only two programs instead of three? We'd do the project in smaller steps but it would still be highly worthwhile."

"I need a much bigger cut than that. Suppose you start with just one program and assign to it the part-time person on your staff who's working on your lowest priority project. Could you then cut this to twenty thousand?"

"That would reduce it too far. We wouldn't be giving the project a fair chance, and we might conclude wrongly that it's no good, when it's really great. I'd say that the smallest worthwhile test would cost twenty-five thousand. Based on our own people's responses, I think it's going to be a big success."

"Okay, draw up a detailed plan with a cost breakdown, and we'll take a look."

Staying Flexible

While you should work out beforehand what your maximum and minimum are, don't set them too firmly. As you work with an idea, your perception of it changes. You realize more about it through the new connections you keep making in thinking about it. In negotiating, your valuing of what you're giving up and getting continues to change. This in turn changes your maximum and minimum. The other person experiences the same flux in his perceptions.

Stay loose. Allow this changing to go on. The more you work with an idea, the clearer it becomes. If you lock yourself into some position, you may lose a deal and regret it later.

Similarly, keep in touch with your feelings. Are you irritated because the other person seems stubborn and unfair? Keep in mind that he's doing what he feels is best for him, just as you are, for you. Are you anxious that he's going to be angry at you for frustrating him? That, too, works both ways.

Are you afraid that you're going to lose the deal if you don't settle now instead of making another offer? Deciding either way involves some risk. You risk losing the deal or you risk getting worse terms than you could have had. It's a gamble since there's no way to tell for sure how the other person will react. So relax and enjoy it. You'll likely perform better.

‖ 14 ‖ Selling Your Ideas in Writing

Why We Have Trouble with Writing

Businesspeople complain that the writing they receive is unintelligible. They can't make out what the writer means. The ideas are disorganized and incompletely worked out. The writers seem to be foundering in a sea of words and trying to save themselves either by writing too little or too much.

Some of the businesspeople probably suspect that there's a vast conspiracy to keep information from them by making writing inscrutable. The more suspicious ones may even imagine that the writing is really a code containing a hidden espionage message. But then they're probably baffled by how crudely the spies disguise the message since the businesspeople can't even understand the disguise.

Businesspeople wonder why the same people who can talk about what they mean can't handle the writing of it. If a person can explain something through talking, why can't he use the same words to explain the same ideas in writing? What's the mysterious barrier in many people that impedes the great leap from talking to writing?

Generally, there is no deep psychological block or hidden aversion to writing. It's just much harder to write than to talk. Since writing makes more demands on a person's abilities than talking does, many people either are unwilling to meet these demands or are frightened by them and become immobilized.

What are these demands? First, writing requires that you think through the whole of what you want to say before you write a word. You have to do this in order to realize what your essential point is and how to organize your material. Doing this demands sustained thought as you work out all the parts, move them around in your mind, and relate them to each other.

Talking about your ideas is much easier since you only have to develop a remark at a time. The other person's remarks guide you in organizing your material since you're responding to his questions and objections as he raises them.

Second, in writing you have to make sure that you're expressing yourself clearly. The reader is not there to ask you questions. Since your familiarity with your idea makes it easy for you to overestimate your clarity, you run the risk of leaving something out.

After sending my literature to a prospect for my services, I received a letter from her expressing interest and saying that she was looking forward to talking with me. Since I couldn't tell whether she was inviting me to call her or saying that she intended to call me, I played it safe and called her. When I explained to her assistant that I was calling because of the ambiguity, he admitted that he wrote the letter for her, now saw my reason for calling, and that he meant that she would call me since she was still perusing my literature.

Third, in writing you have to abide by rules of grammar and punctuation, and watch your spelling. Fourth, writing requires more physical effort, which makes it more tiring. Fifth, it's more difficult to hold on to your thoughts when writing since writing lags behind thinking to a much greater extent than talking does. Sixth, you generally feel that you have to be more careful about what you put in writing. And seventh, you usually require that your writing come up to a higher standard since you have time to plan it and it exists as a whole piece.

Meeting these demands doesn't require any more intelligence, knowledge, or skill than you have. What it does require is patience, self-discipline, effort, and the willingness to risk displaying your writing, which you might feel you're weak in. Actually, you can probably do it much better than you think you can, if you try without holding back.

Thinking Through What You Want to Write

Generally, when you think about the idea you want to sell, you see a mass of problems, benefits, actions to take, costs, risks, and the reactions you anticipate from others. These are tangled up with each other. To put them in writing, you have to untangle them and set them down in a sensible order.

One problem you face is that the reader can read only one word at a time. Yet his mind races ahead trying to form the whole picture before he comes anywhere near finishing reading. He can't relax until he sees where you're heading, so he anticipates it when he's read enough to form something.

A good place to start is with the bottom-line benefit. This captures attention. It also reduces the reader's need to race ahead to see what you're getting at. You can start by saying something like, We can save X dollars or gain Y worker-hours, or produce N more product, or have more skilled or happier employees, or whatever.

After the bottom-line benefit, write your suggested action for getting the benefit. If it feels more comfortable, you can put the suggested action before the bottom-line benefit. In either case, you've started at the end. The reader can see the essence of your idea right off. He doesn't have to guess impatiently at what you're leading to. And you don't run the risk of his forming the wrong mental picture.

To form this opening, you have to think through your whole idea. This means quantifying the benefit where possible, and working out the cost, to arrive at a persuasive cost-benefit ratio. Where you can't quantify, the benefit can still be judged to justify the cost.

Once you have the opening down, you're on your way. You've established your point of departure. From then on you have to show why doing what you suggest will result in the benefit. This means taking the reader from your suggested action through the steps that lead to the bottom line. In doing this, you have to provide evidence that the suggested action is feasible and that each step will occur as you say it will.

Suppose you want to write a proposal to your boss to take the first step in automating the office. How do you begin your proposal? You begin it with the two parts of the bottom line of any proposal: 1. the suggested action and 2. its benefit. To arrive at the bottom line for each of these, you have to think them through and get the facts.

To work out the suggested action and the benefit, you have to answer the following questions: (a) How much should you automate the office? (b) What equipment would you have to buy? (c) How much would the equipment and training cost? (d) How much is the total gain?

After getting the needed facts and doing the calculations to answer these questions, your opening paragraph might be:

> We ought to consider gradually automating the office. Based on some preliminary inquiries I made, if we were to install one word-processing work station for three secretaries to share at a cost of $15,000, we'd get back this investment in

less than a year since we wouldn't have to hire the additional secretary we now need. From then on, we'd save $20,000 a year in salary and fringe benefits. If after three months this work station is successful, we can consider buying an additional work station for each three secretaries. We could reduce our secretarial staff by twenty-five percent.

The reader knows immediately what the writer is proposing. Knowing this prevents the reader from jumping to wrong conclusions. The favorable cost-benefit ratio motivates the reader to read on.

Deciding What to Include

A good way to figure out what to include in your proposal is to put yourself in the place of the reader and ask yourself what you would want to know. In this case, the questions that come to mind are: (a) How would a word-processing station eliminate the need for another secretary? (b) What made you choose this particular word processor? (c) How long does it take to train secretaries to use the equipment, and can they be spared for this amount of time? (d) Would the secretaries' acquiring this extra skill mean that we would have to pay them more? (e) What if the secretaries dislike using word-processing equipment? (f) Have you figured in the costs of the following: maintaining the equipment; higher secretary salaries if needed; and tying up the money for buying the equipment? (g) Which secretaries would operate the first word-processing station? As you answer the questions you first think of, others will occur to you.

You've also got to decide what to leave out. If your proposal is cluttered with unnecessary information, the reader will glance at the voluminous writing, be irritated by the imposition, wonder why the hell you can't say it briefly and to the point, and get an impression that you're disorganized and unable to make sound judgments about how to make a case. It can detract from your image almost as much as does your leaving out information.

You can't decide what to leave out on the basis of whether it's related to the subject. You have to judge this by whether it fits the purpose of the piece you're writing. Since you're proposing buying word-processing equipment to save money, it's premature to make a comparison of the features of the competing models. At this point, you're asking for a decision on only the idea of installing word-processing equipment of some kind. If the other person accepts this idea, your next part would deal with which equipment to buy.

You might be wondering how, then, to answer the second question above: What made you choose this particular word-processing equipment? Wouldn't that call for a comparison of features? No, not in the context of this particular proposal. You need to tell him only enough so that he knows that even if he were to choose a different machine, your proposal is worth looking into.

You would answer it by telling how you went about deciding. You could say that you looked at the features of the various word-processing machines, and determined which features would be worth paying for considering how much you would use them. You then chose the machine with the features you could justify having. But if you were proposing a particular machine, you would then detail the particular features of each machine and its cost, and your expected use of these features.

Staying Relevant

Since irrelevancies can exasperate the reader and turn her against you and your proposal, it's important that you not clutter your writing with them. Some of us have a compulsion to tell everything. One thought leads to another, and it's as though we feel we have to communicate everything in order for the reader to understand anything. Keep in mind that what's relevant is what's necessary to accomplish your purpose.

Before you start writing, you have to decide very specifically what your purpose is. Which of the following are you trying to sell: (a) your investigating whether a particular action should be taken; or (b) your taking that action; or (c) your pursuing a particular way of carrying out that action? Each of these is a further step down the same road than the preceding one. If you aren't clear in your own mind where you're coming in at, you'll blunt your persuasive impact by confusing your reader. You'll spread out your information too much instead of focusing it.

Two or three of these steps can be combined in one proposal just so long as you separate them in your thinking and writing. If you had a growing backlog of work to be done in your unit, you might propose: (a) looking into the problem to find the best solution; or (b) hiring another person with the needed qualifications; or (c) placing a want ad or using an employment agency. You might have already decided to try to sell *b* and want also to advocate a particular form of *c*.

You have to choose your purpose according to what your reader is ready for. You won't be in tune with your reader if you recommend buying a particular model of word-processing machine when she hasn't yet accepted the idea of using word processors. If you're selling the idea of using word processors, you would tell what word processors in general can do but leave describing features of particular word processors to a proposal that recommends a particular model.

Make sure you have a reason for giving each piece of information. It isn't enough to say that you just want to increase the reader's understanding. You have to be able to tell yourself how specifically that piece of information serves the purpose of your proposal.

Maintaining Credibility

The reader wants to know how you arrived at each of your conclusions. He's naturally skeptical since you're asking him to take a risk. Whenever you don't give evidence to support your assertions, he assumes it's because you don't have any such evidence or that the evidence goes against you. Since he attributes motivation to you for whatever you do, if you leave out information, he'll assume you're deliberately doing so.

You have to close all the gaps. Let's consider just one of the questions. How do you know that a word-processing machine will make it unnecessary to hire another secretary? It's because with a word-processing machine a secretary in our business can turn out a third more work. The machine stores the lines of typing that are used repeatedly, and retrieves and inserts them automatically as needed, so that they do not need to be retyped. And letters or words can be changed without having to retype any of the document that contains the change.

How do you know a secretary can turn out a third more work? Because you surveyed the amount of repetitive typing done by a sample of three secreteries and this came to a third of the secretary's work on the average.

How much of each secretary's work did you survey? Because if it was one day's or even one week's work, that may not have been typical. Your sample for each secretary consisted of ten days' work selected at random over the past month. Also, your findings agreed with the testimony of the secreteries that about one-third of their typing is repetitive.

How you know something is so is one of the most important pieces of information for maintaining credibility. You should include it for each assertion you make. The reader is likely to wonder about it.

Telling how you know something is so means telling such things as the source of your information, your facts and reasoning, and any assumptions you're making. Look for ways to quantify. Partial quantifying is better than no quantifying. You ought to include also the negatives and why the benefits outweigh them. If you don't cover an objection that occurs to the reader, his interest might very well fall. Since this objection might wash out your proposal, he could be wasting his time.

When doctors give a patient one year to live, it sounds as though the doctors have put together all their information, and gone through some complex mental calculation involving the vast store of information in their minds. If the patient goes on living past the year, you figure the doctors were wrong. They didn't know what they were talking about. And their credibility goes down.

But the doctors didn't make a mistake. They lost credibility needlessly because they didn't tell that they were going on probability. All they had to do was say that ninety percent of the people in the patient's condition last one year. They would not then be held accountable.

Telling how you know is more important when you're writing than when you're talking, because the reader can't ask for your evidence. It's worth it to play it safe by assuming the reader will want to know your basis. If he does, and you haven't included it, a great barrier will come up in his mind. Get into the habit of telling it. Doing so also helps you make sure that you're building a sound case rather than succumbing to an unfounded enthusiasm.

Orienting the Reader

In writing, you're laying out a specific path of thoughts for the reader to follow. Your path goes through a field containing many other paths that intersect with yours all along the way. You want him to stay on your particular path until he comes to your conclusion. As the reader moves down your thought-path, he can see ahead only one word at a time. As an associated thought-path occurs to him, he may start down it thinking it's yours. After reading a little further, he realizes he's taken a wrong turn and has to retrace his steps to find your path. These digressions are burdensome to him and discourage him from reading further.

The reader moves along your thought-path in the dark. Its visibility is very low. Since only one word at a time comes into view, the reader tries to anticipate what's further ahead so he can mentally adjust to the turns and twists. Often, he anticipates wrongly since he does it based on assumptions he makes.

It's helpful to light the thought-path for the reader as far ahead as you can. A good way to do this is to start at the end by first telling your suggested action and bottom-line benefit. While this spotlights the end point to show the reader where he's heading, it doesn't illuminate the path immediately in front. There are ways to do this so that the reader doesn't have to grope or anticipate.

Rather than just having a beacon at the end of your proposal, put beacons along the way wherever you can. Each of your conclusions is a beacon. It sheds light whether it's the conclusion of the whole proposal or just the conclusion of a paragraph. Therefore, start each paragraph with the conclusion of that paragraph. In the paragraph below, the last sentence should be the first.

> Being confined to working on a word-processing machine all day can become boring. Many secretaries who work on these machines miss having their normal diversity of tasks and interaction with people. In fact, there is a high turnover rate among people who do only word-processing. We would not have only one secretary do all the word-processing for each group of three secretaries. We would train all secretaries to use the machine, and each would use it to eliminate repetitive typing.

Don't Overload

Overloaded paragraphs and sentences discourage reading by making it harder for the reader to grasp the content. Each paragraph should cover a topic and each sentence, a thought. At the end of each, the reader exeriences the momentary release of tension that comes with completion. If she has to wait too long, she feels strained.

The overly long paragraph intimidates visually with its massive block of lines. The reader wants the lighter feel of more frequent empty space. She also has only so much patience for a topic. The long solid block suggests that she may have to stay on that topic beyond her interest in it.

Try to keep your paragraphs to about seven typewritten lines or less. If you're getting beyond that, look for where you can start a new paragraph, even if it's only after three or four lines. You might be able to divide your original paragraph into two shorter paragraphs, with each discussing a different aspect of the topic. To do this, you may need to switch around some sentences.

Overloaded sentences stress the reader by requiring him to manage too many thoughts at once. If you have more than three clauses in a sentence, you likely have an overloaded one. A clause is a sub-sentence or mini-sentence and contains a complete thought in itself. A sentence contains one or more clauses.

With multiple clauses, not only do you have a number of thoughts to hold on to but you also have to master all the relationships among them. You might want to explain that what you're telling in the first clause occurs after, or because of, or in spite of, or seems to contradict, or depends on, or is in addition to, what happened in the second. You use the appropriate words to express this. With all these happenings in the same sentence, your writing becomes dense. Working it out may be too demanding for the reader, and he might just abandon it.

Look how difficult it is to hold on to the following sentence:

> While we could save money initially by buying less expensive word-processing equipment and training only one secretary to operate it instead of training them all, and having one do all the repetitive typing for the three of them, we're likely to lose more in the long run by sacrificing time-saving features that this equipment has, from the increased turnover of the trained secretaries because of boredom, and from the lack of use of the equipment when the trained secretary is absent, resulting in either overtime from having to type the repetitive material on a standard typewriter, or in lateness of documents containing repetitive material since the work load of the group of three secretaries would have been increased because of the increased productive capacity resulting from the word-processing equipment.

You can't fully understand a sentence until you've read all of it because something at the end may affect the meaning of an earlier part. Therefore, to make sense of it you have to hold on to the whole thing until you get to the end, to see how the parts fit together. With a long, dense sentence you have to read it over and over to absorb it. Often, people would rather not read it at all. As a guide, try to limit a sentence to three clauses.

Density results also from a compression of thoughts. If you string too many thoughts together one after the other with too few words for each, there isn't enough time between them to comprehend one before encountering the next. The whole thing becomes a blur. Again, you have to read it over and over. Consider the following sentence:

> The advantages of this particular model are its economy, ease of operation, reliability, appearance, versatility, and reputation.

These six concepts are so crowded together that there's no time to absorb one before the next is on you. Try looking away from this page and seeing how many of the six concepts you can remember. If the reader likes to absorb thoroughly, he'll find himself looking back and reading them over again, perhaps several times, trying to figure out the significance of each as you mean it. This is frustrating since he doesn't have enough information to get a useful picture. He's wasting time speculating, and this discourages him from reading on.

It would be much better to spread out these concepts, by elaborating a little. This gives the reader time to think about them, and to see if more information is needed so that he knows what you mean. The following presentation of the six concepts is easier to absorb:

> This model's price and the cost of its service contract are about ten percent less than others with the comparable features that make it useful for many different applications. It has a reputation for little maintenance, and customers I've talked to say that the supplier provides prompt, competent service. People who have shopped around say that their secretaries find it easy to read the screen and use the controls. They also preferred its compact, streamlined look and subdued color.

Try to Put the Effect Before the Cause

In our discussion of just about anything, we frequently tell that certain things cause other things to happen. In doing so we generally proceed from cause to effect, as in the following: If everyone wouldn't lunch at the same time, the cafeteria wouldn't be too crowded. Getting word-processing equipment will help us keep up with our increased workload. We need to get our people to listen to each other more so that we'll gain more good ideas and make fewer mistakes.

However, the effect is usually more significant to the reader or listener than the cause is. He wants to know right off what's going to result. It's usually better to put the benefit, which is the result, before the suggested action, which is the cause. Telling a person what he'll gain motivates him to find out what he has to do to gain it.

While it's generally more motivating to tell the effect first, you have to consider another rule: Tell first whichever is shorter. If you can tell the cause in a few words, and have to explain the effect much more fully, put the cause first. Don't keep the reader or listener in suspense. Suspense belongs in fiction, where you can identify with characters and enjoy adventures vicariously. But when you're trying to understand ideas, any delay in grasping them is frustrating. When you put the shorter one first, the reader encounters the other part sooner. This gives him a quick grasp of the whole.

Put first whichever is markedly shorter, the cause or the effect. But if they're anywhere near the same length, start with the effect. Perhaps we tend to communicate cause first because that means moving forward chronologically. That's the order in which we live and the order of events in a story. But to evaluate a proposal, the reader wants to see the bottom line first. In every cause-and-effect relationship, the effect is its bottom line. In a proposal, a set of mini–bottom lines leads to the end bottom line.

These are guides rather than rules. If it feels awkward to put either the effect or the shorter part first, don't do it. But try using these guides, and where it feels right, follow them.

Making Your Language More Active

Verbs are vigorous. They act. They don't just sit there; they do something. They make the reading easier to grasp, and they carry the reader along. Instead of saying "He made a presentation," say "He presented." "She felt" rather than "She had the feeling." "He gained" rather than "He made a gain." "He strengthened" rather than "He increased the strength."

Don't look to turn all nouns into verbs. You still need subjects and objects. The nouns to look to are those that you're using in combination with verbs to describe the action. Those nouns you can generally turn into verbs that replace the verb-noun combinations, as shown above.

Another way to get more action in your language is to use the active rather than the passive voice of a verb. Instead of "The most sales were made by the North-Central region," put "The North-Central region made the most sales." Use "We did the research," rather than "The research was done by us," and "The PR department writes the press releases," rather than "The press releases are written by the PR department."

Be Brief and Direct

Don't overwrite. There's a frequent temptation to write a phrase and then to follow it with another phrase that says the same thing in different words. It's as though after saying it one way, another way occurs to you, so you use both rather than choosing between them. At times, this is effective for emphasis, or to define the first phrase. But often it represents not wanting to give up either phrase.

When you keep up this kind of repeating, such as "He spent his money indiscriminately, was too careless with his funds," you burden the reader with excess verbiage. You might also be breaking a faster rhythm that he'd like to maintain. And you frustrate him by making him wait longer to complete the reading and see the whole.

Overexplaining in your writing annoys the reader not only because he has to read what he already knows but also because you're talking down to him. You're tempted to do this because he can't ask you about what he doesn't understand. If you tend to overexplain in your talking, you're likely to do so in your writing.

Take second looks at what you're writing to see if you can eliminate anything the other person already knows. As you take these second looks, you might also watch for writing you can omit because, while it seems interesting to you, it doesn't help accomplish the purpose of your writing. It might be a point you enjoy making so you force a connection.

You have to decide how much understanding is useful to the reader. It's helpful to put yourself in his place. For each item, ask yourself whether it's worth reading. Reread what you've written, and make a conscious effort to improve it. If it's important, reread it three or four times to edit it further. You'll find that if you're alert, you'll discover in later readings needed changes that escaped you in earlier ones.

‖ 15 ‖ Selling Ideas to Groups

Dealing with the Fear of Addressing a Group

The first time I taught a college class, I paced from one side of the classroom to the other. The students followed me with their eyes, their heads swiveling from left to right and back again as though they were watching a tennis game from a sideline. I don't recall feeling afraid but my nervousness showed in my movements.

We've all seen speakers who have never gotten used to making speeches vibrate their notes as their hands shake. And haven't you observed trouser legs flutter and inappropriate gestures made during a talk? It's as though some threat, visible only to the speaker, sets off the trembling.

Why do people who are at ease when talking to an individual panic when talking to an audience? It's because a group has much greater power to disturb our feelings of self-worth than does an individual. If one person dislikes what we do, we can blame it on something in him that causes him to reject us. After all, you can't please everyone.

But when a group rejects us, we feel that it must be because of something in us. Otherwise, why would a number of people unite on it? These people are different from each other in many ways, but they agree that we're doing poorly. All these people can't be wrong. When it happens, it jars our self-esteem.

If talking to a group makes you anxious, think of yourself as talking to one person. Look at a person in the back of the audience and address her. Then every so often shift to another. If you feel comfortable doing it, move your eye contact more frequently in order to cover more people.

On a feeling level, we tend to react toward ourselves in an all-or-none way. We're either good or bad. There are no degrees of goodness. Furthermore, we don't consider that maybe we're not so great in this but we're real good in that. At the moment, there's just a general feeling of goodness or badness.

You need to remind yourself that even if you don't make an impressive presentation, you're not all bad. You're still bright, hardworking, get along well with people, and achieve in your job.

If the audience doesn't like your presentation, it doesn't mean they think you're no good. It only means that they feel that this particular presentation could have been better in some ways. Also, the chances are most of them probably made some presentations that weren't as good as they'd hoped. And while some of them may have made better presentations than yours, you're likely to have done some things better than they have.

You give yourself a grade on everything you do, based on others' reactions and your own observations. The average of these grades is your total self-grade. Since life goes on, you keep averaging in new grades. By the time you're an adult, you've averaged in so many grades that each additional one makes very little difference. Your expectations are based on the self-grade you've already formed.

A sad thing is that early on you might have experienced

others' perceiving you as failing when you didn't really fail. They just had unrealistic definitions of failure, which they imposed on you. As a result, your self-grade is lower than your capability, and you expect to fail even where you'd be likely to succeed. Expecting to fail frightens you, which impairs your performance and helps fulfill your prophecy.

When your self-doubt assails you, try to stand back and appraise yourself objectively. Do you have enough command of your subject to talk informatively about it? Can you provide examples to make your points clear and interesting? Can you vary your voice so that your delivery isn't monotonous? If so, you've got nothing to worry about. You're capable of giving an effective talk.

Start at the End

When you're selling an idea, begin with a bottom-line opening. Start with the suggested action and bottom-line benefit, and follow with how the suggested action leads to the benefit.

Don't lead up to your point by starting with background information to set the stage. Your audience won't know where you're heading, and because people want to see the point immediately, many of them are likely to jump to the wrong conclusion. Some of these conclusions will be negative. You'll have turned off part of your audience because they're against something you didn't even have in mind.

Keeping the audience in suspense makes for confusion when you're trying to persuade. Suspense is great when you're entertaining by telling a story. But it doesn't belong in the selling of an idea. It's likely to irritate.

People set themselves to respond in ways that fit the situation. When they watch a drama, they're set to imagine themselves as being the characters in the portrayed situations.

Just as we discover what we're like from the way we behave

in real situations, so we imagine what we'd do in the fictional ones. We identify with the characters and experience conflict in the excitement of chasing and being chased; and we laugh at the surprise in the humorous line. The suspense serves the audience's purpose then, and they're attuned to react to it.

But the audience's mental set is very different when you're selling them an idea. Then they're set to learn, to evaluate, and to decide. The very uncertainty that excites them in drama frustrates them now.

Some of you may worry that as soon as you tell them what you want, they're going to stop listening. You're afraid they won't appreciate your idea because you didn't first tell them the background. But remember, the captivating part of your opening is the big bottom-line benefit that they're going to get if they do what you're suggesting. They're going to save money, win people over, increase productivity, make more sales, or whatever else you're promising. Now you've got them wondering how acting on your idea will get them the benefit.

Let's compare an opening that leads up to the point in order to first give background with one that gets right to it. We'll start with a lead-up opening.

"Managers have a lot of responsibility, and are vital to our company's performance and growth. They schedule, instruct, train, motivate, guide, and discipline subordinates, as well as trying to keep them happy in their jobs. There's a lot of employee productivity and turnover at stake in putting the right people in the managerial jobs.

"Not everyone is fit to be a manager. An employee may be tops in his specialty and yet not have the temperament to supervise. He may not be an effective leader or trainer or counselor. He may not be able to, nor want to, keep a number of different things going at once."

By now the audience would be wondering what the speaker is getting at. Why is he telling us all this when he knows we know it? Now listen to an opening that enlightens and motivates immediately.

"We can increase productivity, motivation, and morale by doing a better job of selecting supervisors. If all the managers here would base their selection primarily on capability rather than on seniority, we would not only get much better supervisors, but we also wouldn't be trading first-rate employee specialists for poor supervisors."

Anticipating Audience Resistance

Now that the audience knows what the speaker is proposing, most of them start out resisting to varying degrees. Some oppose completely; others are skeptical but willing to consider it further; and still others are neutral and want to hear more. The speaker is talking to a whole range of resistance that hasn't yet become visible.

This resistance is just the natural reaction of people to others' ideas, particularly those that ask for change. It comes also from competitiveness, which makes some audience members want to feel that the speaker's ideas are wrong. As the speaker talks, and the people listening have a chance to feel their way into her ideas, the resistance lessens.

Another source of resistance is the individual attitude that conflicts with the speaker's idea. This resistance varies over the audience. When the speaker presents an idea, it triggers off unthinking reactions that are long held. Often, the first thing the speaker says is misinterpreted and resisted in a reflex kind of way. The resisting audience member doesn't listen on to hear the total position and supporting arguments. He immediately closes his mind by associating the speaker's idea with one he long ago rejected.

There may be a complex of feelings about the speaker's idea operating within the audience member that he's not even aware of. He may have gotten ahead based on seniority, and feels that he owes allegiance to it. Also, he may be distrustful of, and made anxious by, anything other than an objective basis of promotion. He may be a hard worker who produces well and feels that he should be automatically rewarded for this through advancement, rather than being judged according to his suitability for the next higher position.

He doesn't listen closely to an explanation of how seniority, job performance, and potential can all be combined in the evaluation. Depending on how closed he is, he may gradually open up as he realizes the idea is less threatening than he thought.

Implanting Your Ideas

In planning your talk, keep reminding yourself of the great difference between the audience's comprehending an idea and their assimilating it into their reasoning. When a listener comprehends it, she's just getting hold of the idea so that she can examine it. Then she probes into it to grasp how it relates to other ideas and what its implications are for her.

To do this probing, she often needs more information. To get it, she'll ask questions if she's too impatient to wait to see if you get to it. If resistance is mixed with her uncertainty, she may go after the information by making a negative assumption, and use it to raise an objection. She figures that she'll get the information from your response to her objection.

In any case, to assimilate the idea, the listener has to mentally work with it, try it out in some reasoning, and think about where the idea would take her if she accepts it. Gradually, she makes more and more connections between your idea and her own. The rate of assimilating varies from listener to listener. At any given moment, the audience members differ from each other in the sense they have of your idea.

When someone in the audience asks a question, you often

can't tell what he has in mind by that question since you don't know where he's at in developing his picture of your idea. If you answer his question to fit its literal meaning, you might not be filling in the gap in his mind. He hasn't told you the logic behind his question so it's hard to tell what he specifically wants to know.

If your answer doesn't satisfy him, he may attribute this to your ineptness in linking your thinking with his, or to your evading answering because answering would be unfavorable to you. It might not occur to him that his question isn't clear. Answer his question as best you can and then ask him whether your answer covers his question.

To bring your audience members close to each other in their understanding of your presentation, it's important to repeat frequently without sounding dull. You can do this by giving examples, asking questions that lead them to discuss your ideas, relating something you're saying now to something you said before, and using visuals.

In planning your talk, work out the specific questions and examples you'll use and where you'll place them. Using them gives the group members who are developing their conceptions more slowly, and perhaps more deeply, a chance to catch up with the others. At the same time, it takes the quicker but perhaps shallower idea-graspers further into the ideas.

Keep in mind that those expectant faces waiting for your message do not represent minds contoured like empty cups waiting for wine. Those cups are already full, many with old wine that doesn't mix with the wine of your ideas. Your audience has acquired a strong taste for their old wine. A good part of your selling is to get them to set theirs aside for the moment and try yours. You've got to coax them to taste it and then take a little more, not push them to swallow it all at once.

One of the most important realizations you can come to is that buying an idea is done gradually. Sudden enthusiaism can be quite misleading, for it can go as quickly as it comes. An idea grows slowly like a seed sprouting and spreading roots. Often, the seed of the idea lands in dry, unreceptive soil. There may be lots of rock and little nourishing earth. The idea must be tended, brought along, provided with places for its tendrils to take hold. That's why selling an idea, like gardening, requires so much patience.

The very gradualness of an idea's taking hold means that you can't judge your impact from the audience's immediate reaction. You may have started them thinking in the direction of your idea without their admitting this. Soon, they may ask you more about it; or at another time they may be more receptive to it. Bit by bit they may come to accept it. Your talk, in starting the sale, may have been more successful than you thought.

Organizing Your Speech

Since in your opening you're starting with your final conclusion, you've got to show how you arrived at it. This support is the backbone of your persuasive speech. The selling of your idea depends on how convincing your support is, and on how fully the audience absorbed it in spite of their resistance.

In presenting your opening for your speech recommending selection of managers based mainly on capability rather than on seniority, you immediately raise a number of questions in the minds of the audience. What makes the speaker think they're stressing seniority so much? Since the people with the most seniority in a job are the ones who know it best, shouldn't they be the ones to manage others in it? If people with the most seniority are passed over, what do you do about their loss of morale and motivation? If you try to figure out who's going to make the best manager, aren't you going to make your share of mistakes? And when you do, won't you get a poor manager and look bad yourself, in addition to losing the will to work of the top-seniority person?

In your planning, work out the answers to the questions you think your opening will generate, and present this information next. Your answers will in turn suggest further questions to you that guide you in developing the next portion of information to present.

Questions are not only useful guides to yourself in organizing your speech, but they are valuable, powerful tools when incorporated in your presentation. They keep the audience alert, and make them think about and absorb your ideas. Insert the questions at useful points in the plan of your presentation.

You can use the rhetorical question for its persuasive impact, to lead the audience's thinking. You pose this kind of question without either you or the audience answering it since the answer you intend is obvious. You can raise questions to stimulate reaction to your idea by asking the question, pausing for a moment to allow the audience to go through the automatic response of reaching for an answer, and then answer it yourself. And you can use questions to involve the audience in discussion. After his opening the speaker might say:

> Based on our records, ninety-five percent of the employees who were promoted to manager in this division over the last three years also had the most seniority. While seniority should certainly be considered, this high percentage means that seniority has too much influence.
>
> The person with the most service in a job might seem to be the one to manage others in it since he knows it best. But is managing just a higher level, or more complex version, of the employee's job; or is it a very different kind of job? Isn't the manager planning and scheduling the work of others and guiding and motivating them?
> Choosing a manager on your appraisal of his ability to man-

age has its problems. You might antagonize the passed-over employee who has seniority; and you could make a mistake in selecting the manager.

But isn't the risk of getting a mediocre manager far greater if you let seniority alone make the choice, than if you base it in addition on his potential for managing and also on the characteristics he shows in his present job performance, such as: [the speaker points to each characteristic below on a visual as he tells it] how effectively he learns and solves problems; how hard he works; how well he gets along with others; how much aggressiveness, creativity, and initiative he uses; how open he is to criticism; how fully he plans and looks ahead; what emotional control he has; how decisive he is; and how willing he is to persist and insist when he feels he's right? To complete the picture, you evaluate him for characteristics that are necessary for managing but not for his present job, such as: the ability to train, guide, and motivate subordinates; and the capacity to take a broader view and to plan, schedule, and interpret on a larger scale.

I put these needed characteristics on display up here to emphasize how carefully you have to observe, analyze, and evaluate in order to get the most productive managers. Can we afford to leave it to seniority to do this for us?

Here are some more questions to guide the speaker, suggested by his answers to the previous questions: How do you motivate the passed-over employee who has seniority? How do you evaluate for those characteristics that a manager needs? The speaker continues his speech by answering these questions.

You're likely to encounter some dejection and a feeling of being treated unfairly from the employee who was passed over. How can you keep him motivated and productive? Well, for one thing, you can add the word *senior* to his title.

You can discuss his feelings with him to let him vent them. Explain that his abilities are much more suited to performing his specialty than to managing others in performing theirs. He's very valuable in what he does and would be much less valuable as a manager. One person is better at doing the job itself, and another person is more capable in getting others to do it well. You might also suggest to the manager that at times he ask the senior employee for his opinion and bring him in on meetings where useful. Does anybody have any other suggestions about how to handle this problem? [If this question succeeds in involving the audience in working on this problem, the speaker has them moving toward buying his idea.]

Let's take up how to evaluate employees for the characteristics I've listed up here. You can rate each employee on each characteristic that he applies to his present job. You can keep a chart and update it every six months. Meanwhile, during that time note incidents that involve these characteristics to support your evaluation.

To evaluate the characteristics that are more specific to managing, assign those you feel are likely candidates to train and guide new employees. You can then note how well the candidates instruct and motivate.

Each candidate will rate higher on some characteristics than on others. From the ones who rate highly enough on all the needed characteristics to be considered for the manager position, choose the one who has the most seniority. Isn't this a useful way of combining present performance, potential for managing, and seniority in your selecting the person for the manager job? And aren't we likely to get better managers this way than if we relied on seniority alone?

Handling Questions from the Audience

Questions from the audience contribute greatly to your talk's effectiveness. For one thing, they clear up the inevitable information gaps that occur because things that seem clear to you aren't clear to all of them. Second, their questions make your talk more dramatic. The audience listens to different ideas, different personalities, and different voices.

Furthermore, if someone in the audience challenges you, excitement is added. On a radio talk show I participated in, the host encouraged the guests to argue with each other. Controversy sparks interest.

You can either invite the audience to raise a question whenever they wish, or you can provide for a question period at the end. The first way makes your talk more lively, and enables the audience to follow you better if they can clear up questions as they occur rather than leaving the questions hanging until the end. It also brings you closer to the audience since you're interacting with them.

However, if you have too little time for all the information you want to impart, better leave the questions for later. But before you give up the advantage of answering questions as you go along, see if you can cut down on your information instead. Pick out the essential concepts you're trying to sell and drop out what isn't really necessary. Besides, you might be able to work in more information in your answers to their questions. But even if you can't, you can often do a better job of selling by trying to sell fewer ideas but repeating them more. Questions provide a stimulating way of repeating, and also involve the audience.

To keep your credibility high, answer questions directly. Start your answer with its essential point. Don't begin by qualifying or explaining or leading up. Do that after you give your direct answer.

The essential point of the answer to a "yes-no" question is a yes, no, or I don't know; to an "how much" question is the quantity; and to a "when" question is the date, time, or time relationship to some other event. Begin your answer to a "why" question with the word *because*; and to an "how-can-something-be-done" question with the word *by*. Using these words to begin leads you right to the essential point.

Immediately after saying the essential point, give your supporting evidence. Tell what makes you think it's so. Doing this raises your credibility. It shows you've done your homework. You are not making unsupported assertions.

Let's watch the speaker handle some questions from the audience:

> Suppose the person with the most seniority has high enough ratings to qualify him for the manager position, but another person with less seniority has higher ratings. He looks like he'd make a better manager. Which person do you choose?

> The one with the most seniority. After all, your rating system isn't perfect. It's a good guide but you could be interpreting for the needed characteristics differently from how they would be applied in the manager job. Considering also the problem of maintaining morale, it seems worthwhile to go by seniority as long as the most senior person has the needed qualities.

> If I have a lower seniority person who is eager to get ahead, with higher capability than the senior person has, although the senior person has enough capability, and I promote on the basis of seniority, aren't I likely to lose the ambitious, highly capable person?

> Yes, that's certainly possible. You could take steps to counteract this. You could let him know that you're well aware of his talent and are keeping him in mind for a manager position; but since the senior person is also qualified, you felt you should promote him. He does have solid experience, knows the job thoroughly. Even if the capable person quits, could you have been sure that he would have worked out as a manager? It's still a matter of probabilities. Meanwhile, you might lose the senior person either by his leav-

ing, or through faltering productivity because of his disappointment.

If you don't have confidence in your ratings, what's the good of using them? You might as well go by seniority.

I do have a certain amount of confidence in the ratings. It isn't a question of either absolute confidence or no confidence. You can have high confidence in your ratings if you make them carefully and base them on evidence you've accumulated on the employee's behavior. But you can't be certain. The reason for using them is that combining them with seniority results in a selection decision that's right far more often than using seniority alone is when selecting managers.

Dealing with Resistance

When someone in the audience opposes your idea and some others back him up, it may feel as though the whole audience is slipping away from you. You feel outnumbered. The power of the group is getting to you. You have the feeling that the silent others in the audience support the vocal ones.

But it's not that way. Since unreasonable resistance to others' ideas is natural, and this resistance varies in strength over the audience, you're bound to encounter both vocal and silent opposition that has little to do with the merits of your idea. You've got to patiently stay with it. The resistance gradually diminishes as the audience gets used to your idea.

Your anxiety leads you to exaggerate the resistance of the silent ones. They come around without any visible shifting of their attitudes. One or two of them may argue in your favor against some objections. This is a sign that you're reaching more people than you realize. Another sign is others' asking real information-seeking questions rather than argumentative ones. We're assuming here that your ideas make sense, are well supported, and don't run counter to the basic values of the group.

When someone raises an objection ("Keeping records on everybody as a basis for the ratings would take up too much time. We've got too many other things to do."), at least some of the force behind it is unreasonable resistance. For if she were open to the idea but reasonably concerned about the cost, she would raise her concern in the form of a question. ("How would we keep these records of incidents to make ratings so that it doesn't take up too much time?")

Feelings against your idea can be generated in her by her competitiveness, negative reactions to you, conflict between your idea and some of her basic beliefs, current frustrations, her needing more time to assimilate your idea, or her fear of risk or change.

In responding to an objection, you're talking one-to-one. You're selling that individual in the presence of the rest of the group. Your response also influences the thinking of others who have the same concern. And the directness, clarity, and reasonableness of your reply contribute to the whole group's image of your credibility and competence. This in turn affects how they receive your message.

Since you are talking one-to-one, for the moment, you would use the technique models for responding to an objection. This means using either an inquiry into the other person's reasoning, or a constructive inquiry. You can't extend the inquiry for more than one or two remarks. If you do, you might lose the interest of the rest of the group. While you don't have the time to get a commitment from him that he has given up his objection, your brief inquiry can get him to question the objection himself. Let's watch the speaker use inquiries to deal with objections raised by an audience member.

If I don't promote the person with the most seniority, I'll have someone who's unhappy and unproductive. He'll infect the whole department with his grumbling. That would just put a big burden on me.

Yes, an unhappy employee who doesn't produce might lower morale. Couldn't you with a combination of counseling and broadening his participation in problems and meetings gradually get him to accept the situation? If necessary, you could transfer him to a different job where he would have fresh experiences. Wouldn't your problem be far greater if you acquired a poor manager who lowered the productivity of everyone under him?

Of course it would. But I would train him, send him to courses in managing. I'd make him into a good manager.

That would certainly be worthwhile if it could be done. But aren't there a number of employees for whom training wouldn't work? They just don't have the basic capability for managing. If you feel the employee with the most seniority can be developed, by all means promote him. All I'm asking you to do is to make sure he has the needed qualities, so that training will make the difference. As a guide, you can ask yourself if he's likely to turn out to be a manager that you feel you could work under.

This is as far as the speaker can pursue this objection without having others in the group tune out. The chances are that the inquiry questions will make the audience member think enough about his objection to give it up then, or at a later time, after he has thought more about the problem.

When the resistance takes the form of hostility, it can be unsettling; particularly if it comes from a number of people at the same time. The danger is that it might make the speaker anxious or angry and cause him to either back off or else attack the audience. One particularly provoking form of hostility is ridicule. Someone in the group might say to the others:

Listen, here's what he means. All you need to say to the guy that was passed over is that not making him a manager is for his own good. He'd be unhappy, and you didn't want to make him unhappy, so you chose some other unlucky person. [He turns to the speaker.] Right? Isn't that what you meant?

If the speaker gets flustered or angry, he'll be inviting more taunts or other attacks from the audience. While some in the group are likely to support him, others will vent their anger, disrupting the speech. Whether the attack is a direct one or takes the form of sarcasm, the speaker needs to defuse the situation by sympathizing and staying calm and reasonable. He might say:

I wish it were that easy. I know what you're up against and it's hard to face. I haven't got any easy answers. If you're going to be stuck with a problem either way, isn't it better to make the best of it by doing what gives you the smaller problem? And isn't having a bad manager a worse problem than dealing with a person who's been passed over?

Controlling Your Own Resistance

When someone in the group resists your idea, your own resistance could affect your response without your realizing it. Your resisting can turn off your audience. And unless you become sensitive to it, it's hard to see your own resistance. You'll seem dogmatic, closed-minded, as though you're not actively listening. You've got to watch yourself, continually take readings of your own reactions to make sure you're flexible, inquiring, rather than being unyielding and rebutting. Suppose someone in the audience says:

I don't know where you get this idea that your method is better than seniority for choosing a manager. I know one person who chose on the basis of performance and capability and wound up with a manager who's screwing up his unit. Another person, who went by seniority, got himself a great manager. So you can't say one way is better than another. Maybe each of us ought to use the way that's most comfortable and works best for him.

Now watch the speaker become dogmatic:

No, that's no good. You just wind up going by seniority. You've got to make an effort, try it where you evaluate performance and potential. You've got to take the risk.

The speaker would have shown more open-mindedness by saying:

It's true that at times seniority works fine and using your evaluation of an employee results in a poor manager. But wouldn't you expect that most of the time, observation and evaluation combined with seniority will work better than seniority alone does?

Another way the speaker might reveal her own resistance is by answering a question too quickly, without finding out what the audience member has in mind by his question. Why is he asking? As a result, the speaker might sound like she's trying to impose her thinking on the audience rather than trying to fit her thinking to theirs. Suppose an audience member asks the following:

Do you think we really know enough about what makes a good manager, and how to tell if someone has the needed qualities for managing?

If the speaker is resisting, she's likely to give a flat answer such as:

Yes, I do. Some of you can do better than others, but you'll all generally do better than going by seniority alone.

First of all, the speaker can't be sure of what's behind that question. Is the audience member thinking, Since we don't know enough, how can we tell who will make a good manager? Or is he wondering whether he can get some training in choosing a manager? Second, the speaker hasn't told what she bases her answer on. She just asserts it. The speaker would have shown more responsiveness by saying:

Yes, I think you know enough about what's needed to be a good manager since you're managers yourselves. But if you feel you'd like more knowledge of this, we can certainly discuss it. Also, there's plenty of reading material on it in our library. How to tell if someone has the needed qualities is a different problem. To do this, it's important to systematically observe, note down, analyze, and evaluate right along so that you have the information when the time comes to decide. If the senior person doesn't have the needed qualities, you can evaluate the next senior person. Perhaps we ought to have a meeting on how to do this. Did you have something particular in mind in asking that question?

The audience member then says:

Well, I was wondering how we could increase our skill in selecting managers. Is there a course we could take?

And the speaker responds:

Yes, we could set up a workshop in this. How do the rest of you feel about having such a workshop?

Holding Your Audience

A monotonous voice causes listeners to tune out. Since we adapt to stimuli that impinge on our senses in a steady, unvarying way, we stop perceiving the constant tone, sight, and odor. It's to counteract this adaptation response that sirens rise and fall in pitch and advertising signs go on and off.

Besides, there are many inner thoughts and feelings trying to pull away our attention. As soon as a speaker relaxes his stimulation of our senses, we drift, unaware that we've mentally left. Then when there's a letup in our inner demands, we suddenly realize that we've been away for a little while. To hold attention, you've got to do with your voice what the rising and falling siren, and the blinking sign, do. Varying your pitch and volume is essential to hold attention. And this variation has to be meaningful, not done at random. It's to highlight certain points for emphasis.

Beyond this, many people need to raise the level of excitement in their voices. This excitement not only keeps stimulating the hearing sense to prevent tune–out but also gives the feeling that you care very much. This compels listening because it makes the information sound important.

Often, people speak monotonously because their voices sound to them much more exciting than they sound to their audiences. When a person speaks, he hears the variations in his voice intensity as though they were magnified, because the sounds reverberate in his head. To his audience, these variations diminish as they cross the intervening space.

Also, to varying degrees, many people who associate an enthusiastic voice with expressing feelings also are afraid to express their feelings. Some fear that if they do, feelings that seem unacceptable will be revealed. They underestimate their self-control. Others are afraid that if they sound excited, they'll lose their image of being calm and thoughtful.

As a result, they're afraid to venture into making their voices more dramatic. Furthermore, they see no need to do so since they hear the excitement magnified and that's as intense as they need to be.

It's an enlightening experience to listen to a tape recording of your speech. What you hear is how it sounded to your audience; much more toned down than it sounded to you while you were saying it. Now, try a little experiment. Record a small portion of the talk you plan to give, saying it in a very excited manner. Raise this excitement to the point where it feels embarrassing to deliver a speech so intensely. You're likely to find when you listen to the tape that your voice sounds quite normally interesting and not at all overly intense.

To get into the habit of talking in a voice that captures attention, provide yourself with frequent feedback. Experiment when you're alone by recording your reading aloud, or giving a talk, with varying degrees of excitement. Note how much more exciting your voice sounds as you say it, than the way it comes back on the tape. Gradually, you'll get the feel of how to adjust your voice so it sounds to others the way you want it to.

Another useful exercise is to record a radio commercial. Then write it out and record yourself reading it. Compare your reading of it with that of the announcer's. Then record it while trying to reach his level of excitement. You may be amazed at how absurdly excited you feel reading it, and yet how normal it sounds when you listen to it on the tape.

Making Sense with Gestures and Movements

Many people use their hands when they talk, as though the words alone don't convey the meaning. Their hands seem to be trying to shape meaning more precisely. Perhaps the hand movements are also a way of letting out feeling.

A speaker often repeats the same gesture rhythmically. These movements probably discharge the tension built up in the attempt to instill the exact meaning in others' minds. A certain frustration probably builds up in trying to find the right combination of words to express exactly what he thinks and feels. And there's often some doubt that others have an understanding that parallels his.

Rhythmic hand gestures can disturb others. Since movement of any kind automatically draws attention, it takes away from thinking about the meaning coming across. This distraction occurs because the gestures are not synchronized with the words. The hand movements take place as a separate activity. And while they arise from the speaker's thoughts and feelings, they carry no message to the audience.

Hand gestures and body movements should be made to carry the same meaning as the verbal message does, or to tell that something being said is particularly important. To do this, the speaker should use hand gestures purposefully. The hand gesture introduces a change in the visual field, and this captures attention. This attention should be drawn to the verbal message rather than away from it.

Let's watch the speaker integrate his gestures and movements with his comments:

You may feel that in choosing by seniority, you're cutting out your risk. [The speaker puts his right hand at the left side of his chest, palm down and fingers outstretched and together, and as he says the last part of the sentence, he thrusts his hand outward and toward the right, slicing the air.] But are you reducing the right risk? You're eliminating the risk that the senior person will be angry at you and dejected, and lose his motivation. But is this the risk to be more concerned about [thrusts his left hand out pointing toward the left]? Or is the more important risk that of getting a poor manager [thrusts right hand out pointing to the right]?

[To suggest that something he is about to say is particularly illuminating, the speaker moves a few steps closer to the audience.] Let me ask you something. If you were an employee in a work group, would you want your next boss to be selected by seniority, or would you prefer to work for someone chosen because he has leadership ability, listens and is responsive to others' needs, and knows how to guide and motivate? Under which one would you reach out to do more [reaches out his right hand with fingers open as though he were trying to grasp something]?

Getting Valuable Support from Visuals

In addition to using your own body as a visual, through gestures and movements, visuals you create can add much to making your presentation clearer and more interesting. They can also distract. It depends on whether your visuals supplement or compete with you, and how understandable they are.

Your visual competes when it presents the same information you do, simultaneously with your presenting it. While the audience studies the visual, it misses what you're saying; when they shift to you, they miss what the visual contains. At any given time, some audience members are listening to you while others are attending to the visual.

Your visuals should provide an alternate mode of communicating. When you're using the visual, talk about it. Don't just leave it there to function on its own while you talk independently about your ideas. An effective way of talking about the visual is to ask questions whose answers are contained in the visual. You can answer the questions yourself, pointing to the answers in the visual, or you can invite the audience to answer.

Suppose you were using a bar graph that showed how employees rate the importance to them of various characteristics of their managers (is fair, criticizes constructively, is willing to listen). Rather than talking generally about the relative importance of each of the various characteristics needed for successful managing, and leaving the bar graph to show this independently, talk specifically about the bar graph and what it means. You might ask the group how their ratings compare with those on the bar graph.

Don't use a visual just to have one. If the visual serves no purpose, it seems as though you could have thought of a better one but didn't bother. Actually, you may not have needed a visual at all. The disadvantage in using a visual is that it divides the audience's focus between you and the visual. You should have a benefit from the visual that's great enough to outweigh the distracting side effect.

Another use for visuals is to provide an organization of the material. Key words or phrases are listed in a display in front of the room so that the audience can anticipate and follow the sequence of topics. The speaker can use this listing so that he doesn't have to look at notes to see what he's to talk about next. The visual is his notes. He can glance at them without losing visual contact with the audience.

Using the Technique Models
to Run Productive Meetings

Meetings don't have to slide into self-expression sessions where most of the participants say their piece, while others are thinking about what they're going to say rather than listening. Instead, the meeting leader can require that the bottom-line opening, the inquiry, and the question-answering technique models be used. This requirement brings a reduction in mutual resistance, and a reasonable thinking together, so that problems are worked on productively and a meeting of minds results.

The leader sets the following ground rules: 1. each person is to use a bottom-line opening to introduce his idea: 2. when someone disagrees with the idea, he has to use an inquiry—acknowledge the merit in the idea and then inquire about the part that he is concerned about; 3. no other idea can be introduced until the idea being discussed is dealt with; 4. anyone asking a question tells why he's asking if it isn't apparent; and 5. anyone asked a question answers it directly and then explains his support for his answer.

The leader reminds the participants of the rules whenever: they start arguing instead of inquiring; they avoid getting right to the point; they don't tell why they're asking a particular question and its purpose isn't clear; or they don't answer questions directly or provide support for their answer.

By applying these concepts and techniques to all your persuasive communications, you can achieve much more for yourself and for your organization. You'll be multiplying the number of good ideas you get into action. And your persuasive interactions will be richer experiences. For you'll be more effective in your thinking, presenting, listening, and responding.

Index

About the Author

Dr. Jesse S. Nirenberg is a consulting industrial psychologist whose office and home are in Scarsdale, New York. He has been conducting in-house and public seminars in persuading and negotiating for over twenty years for major companies and government agencies.

His two previous books have been translated into five languages. His articles have appeared in a number of business publications.

He is a member of the American Psychological Association and the American Society for Training and Development, and is in *Who's Who in the East*. He has a Ph.D. in psychology from New York University, and a Bachelor of Chemical Engineering from Brooklyn Polytechnic Institute.

Catalog

If you are interested in a list of fine Paperback
books, covering a wide range of subjects
and interests, send your name and address,
requesting your free catalog, to:

McGraw-Hill Paperbacks
11 West 19th Street
New York, N.Y. 10011